HEAVENLY TREE,
NORTHERN EARTH

ALSO BY GERRIT LANSING

A February Sheaf
(Pressed Wafer, 2003)

HEAVENLY TREE, NORTHERN EARTH

GERRIT LANSING

NORTH ATLANTIC BOOKS
BERKELEY, CALIFORNIA

Copyright © 2009 by Gerrit Lansing. All rights reserved. No portion of this book, except for brief review, may be reproduced, stored in a retrieval system, or transmitted in any form or by any means—electronic, mechanical, photocopying, recording, or otherwise—without the written permission of the publisher. For information contact North Atlantic Books.

Published by
North Atlantic Books
P.O. Box 12327
Berkeley, California 94712

Dustjacket illustrations:
from *Geheime Figuren der Rosenkreuzer, aus dem 16ten und 17ten Jahrhundert* (Altona, 1785–88). Courtesy University of Wisconsin Digital Collections.

Dustjacket and book design by Jonathan Greene

Printed in the United States of America

Heavenly Tree, Northern Earth is sponsored by the Society for the Study of Native Arts and Sciences, a nonprofit educational corporation whose goals are to develop an educational and cross-cultural perspective linking various scientific, social, and artistic fields; to nurture a holistic view of arts, sciences, humanities, and healing; and to publish and distribute literature on the relationship of mind, body, and nature.

North Atlantic Books' publications are available through most bookstores. For further information, visit our Web site at www.northatlanticbooks.com or call 800-733-3000.

Library of Congress Cataloging-in-Publication Data

Lansing, Gerrit.
 Heavenly tree, northern earth / Gerrit Lansing.
  p. cm.
 ISBN 978-1-55643-754-0
 I. Title.
 PS3562.A5617H37 2009
 811'.54—dc22
                              2009011444

1 2 3 4 5 6 7 8 9 SHERIDAN 14 13 12 11 10 09

CONTENTS

I. INSCRIPTIONS

The Heavenly Tree Grows Downward   3
To Her of Solemn Music   4
For an Unlikely Love   5
A Poem of Love in Eleven Lines   6
Eine Kleine Nachtmusik nach Likymnius   7
The Welcome   8
A Toast   10
Graffiti, Ancient and Modern   11
Formula to Get By With   12

II. REMINDERS

The Great Form Is Without Shape   15
Stephen Phillips and the Warmth of Summer Nights   17
The Green Bottle   23
A Red Ghazel for C.B.L.   24
From Under the Mat Where Sat the Cat   25
The Milk of the Stars from Her Paps   26
The Glory of Changes   33

III. EXPLORERS

An Inlet of Reality, or Soul   41
Cleaving Making Rock   42
Hands that Melt Like Snow   44
Tea at Slinky's Palazzo   45
Bracketing in City Thickets   47
Judgment of the City   48
The Dark Grammarian   49

The Malefic Surgeon   50
3 Poems of the Underworld(s)   51
3 Anecdotes of the Uncanny   54
Prose for St. Catherine's Day   57
In the Grip of the Octopus   58
Explorers   59

IV. WORKING IN THE LOWER RED FIELD

Working in the Lower Red Field   63
Perianth   64
One of the Company of Light   66
The Castle of Flowering Birds   67
To Wee Virgins to Make Much of Time   68
Makes the Mind Grow Duller   69
Wild Cherries   70
The Conditioned   71
A February Mind Hung Untimely Up in Summer's Weave   72
A Ghazel of Absence   73
I See Bright Sun Illuminating Absence   74
Song: *L'Amour est echoué*   75
Thinking of the Eyebrows of My Lord   76
Alba   77
The Recluse (fragment)   78
Amphion   & His Song   79
Boxcar Moonlight Scene   80
A Comfort in the Longing Flames   81
Love Poem   82
How We Sizzled in the Pasture   83
The Joint is Jumping   85
Melanthus in the Mountains   86
Romanza   87
History   89
Needfire   91
Going Green in the Fall   92
The Unsealing   93

V. A PLACE

Planting the Amplitudes   97
Blue Decrepit Town   98
Honey from the Rock   100
New Commentary on an Old Tune   101
Dusky   103
Sunset as Early Warning System   104
Abbadia Mare   105
Postcard on Henry David   107
The Curve   108
A Simple Fire of Wood   111
The Boulder Behind the House   112
Strolling Pebble Beach in February   114
Annisquam Nights   115

VI. SOME GONE

A Far Memory of Lazy Spring   119
Dead Man Blues   120
The Bereft   121
Amazing Grace and a Salad Bowl   123
Furiously Framing, Stephen Jonas Jauntily   127
For John Wieners, 1934–2002   128
from The Orchards of Sleep   129
Elegiac Fantasy, Delayed in Glass   134
Skeleton Echo   136
August Desolation Ply   137
Auguries in Autumn   138
October Song   139

VII. ON EARTH, PARTICULAR

Weed Udana   143
Red Flowers in the Kitchen   144
Egg Breakfast   145
Ballet   146

The Red-Mouthed Green Parrot   147
On the Right Use of Simples   148
To the Boy Charioteer   149
In the Light of the Tinctures   151
Gold Coast Tanka   153
Today   154
A Drink   155
Habits   156

VIII. PERISHING REPUBLIC

The Wizard of Oz in the Blizzard of Oz   159
The Compost   167
In the American Forest   169
Good Goo in Sooth   171
Reading "My Life" on a Greyhound Bus from Boston to New York   173
Will Glen Burnie Never Pass Away?   175
Portrait of a Poetaster, and Gentleman of Ample Means   176
Quatrain for Contemporary "Amazing Grace" Stanza Collection   177
The Undertaking   178

IX. PORTALS

In Erasmus Darwin's Generous Light   181
Stanzas of Hyparxis   185
When Locality Fails   193
Conventicle   194
Tabernacles   195
Rumors   196
The Belt   197
Festival Song (the New Year)   198
Song (the Autumn Festival)   199
Equinoctiall (1)   200
Equinoctiall (2)   201
The Cutting of the Lotus   202
Olana   204
The End of Nature in this World   210

Cinquain: Bethel   211
The Many-Worlds Interpretation   212
The Gold in the Mud   213
Ialdobaoth   214
The Ogdoad   215
Enthymeme   216
Behind the Vale and in the Pleasaunce of the Pythagorean Comma   220
Without Design Design Goes On   225
Finding the Flap   227

X. THE SOLUBLE FOREST

The Soluble Forest   231

XI. IN NORTHERN EARTH

In Northern Earth   255

APPENDIX: THE BURDEN OF SET

Statement: How *Set* Was Conceived   259
The Burden of Set #1 (editorial   261
The Burden of Set #2 (editorial   267

I.

INSCRIPTIONS

THE HEAVENLY TREE GROWS DOWNWARD

Who bury the dead
must from the grave
establish a habit

Who bury the dead
lead forth the bride
stainless in dress

the morning-
glory creeps
stone
lizard

Who bury the dead
in fetal position
knees pulled up to chin

Who bury the dead
to rise again

TO HER OF SOLEMN MUSIC

The ruin of dedication

is a ruin of my heart,

broken obelisk of caring past

the past obliquities of love.

Once gone down the hell hole

there is no turning back,

golden reversion.

What time, meaning age, has once disposed,

She ever disposes ever.

My loves, all my selfishness

               monuments

                            of agony

                                        pass

to where the god has willed and willed again

               my pain and out of body bliss.

Great Woman, give me courage.

FOR AN UNLIKELY LOVE

I praise the canyons no bridge spans

but eagles fly across.

A POEM OF LOVE IN ELEVEN LINES

Dreamer of purified fury and fabulous habit,
your eyes of deserted white afternoons
target, stiffen, riot with unicorn candor
so I swallow your body like meanings or whisky or as you swallow me.

Break rhythm here: your kiss is my justice:
look then now how orange blooms of jubilation unfold in satisfied air!
This sex is more than sex, under the will of the God of sex,
so I softly invoke transformation of your rueful image of haven
—those frozen rocks, that guilty lighthouse isolate from temptation—
to warm Flemish landscape green and brighteyed with daisies of
    dizzying color
where pilgrims are dancing after gospelling birds who sing of
    new springs, good water.

EINE KLEINE NACHTMUSIK NACH LIKYMNIUS

or

'call it nothing but a memory'

Dark Hypnos so loves the freshness of your glance,

    Endymion divinely disarranged upon my couch,

        the God gives you to dream with eyes open all night long.

THE WELCOME
for Nerval, *le pendu*

weightless

                                                    in the cold wind

           ("I am thirsty")

                                                   of angels

the old lantern dim

                     between the sewers'   entrance

                     in the cold wind and snow

(a mummy in a glass coffin plumbed the time... Wednesday,
                                    Jan. 26, 1855,
    Pluto squaring Sun)

without an overcoat
              the street of the old lantern dim
in the fury of cold and heavy night

        (come to me my boy, don't wait to end the night)
            52   4x13

                 beckoning

                 again returned
having three times plunged into the icy stream

            stopped by the cops in Baudoyer Square

                           released

    he wandered
       into the region called the Ancient Butcheries

  misery's valley   odor of dried blood

where the familiar turned its head and closed its eyes

    he had reached
           the end of music
          and of lights.

("I am involved in a story where I lose my way…"

    Again the crow spoke: *J'ai soif.*

Gerard unwound the sacred string   said a word he knew

  and opened the door for glory…

      It was the thirteenth hour.

A TOAST

(suggested by Mallarmé's *Salut*)

to *Poesy*

for Robin Blaser

hey   salvific toot

        or
hail
        festival and verse,
        designate the plunging chalice
        whose so far upside down sirenical
         your Yes-of-Nay eventuates

                foam
        of funest winter lightning.
        You raise for us such solitude,
        unshipwrecked star of care
        and unbelief our whitest joyous words.

GRAFFITI, ANCIENT AND MODERN

Poised in classic haunts of failure,
Take formal solace, pensive eye,
In "fragments of a faith forgotten,"
Magic of a ruined cult
On ruined walls commended,
                          good
Talismans of mythic port
And habit, sigillary,
                   apt
To testify their archetypes,
Of brilliant earth the primitives.

Hermetic, terrible from joy,
A rude imagination blazed
This iconography, not
To animate the game of nerves
Nor galvanize a rotting fiber,
But, as supernatural,
To lead the florid intellect
Through lovely glades of calm conceiving
Until it know its final earth.

Then, *agathadaimon,* fall
Like music from this tainted air,
Involve the will in fairest music
And fair invite the spirit home
Where mirrored in these harmonies
The rapture of itself it views
And how it needs to seem to be.

FORMULA TO GET BY WITH

"I am the son of who don't exist (or don't not exist)

though I exist.   Why I exist,

to mine what's mine and what's not mine (both)

yet what's not mine yes that's mine (partly)

since they belong to my female friend my female side

who made them for herself I call her wisdom.

But I existed

            thanks to beyond-it-daddy who don't,

and now me go back where I really belong."

II.

REMINDERS

THE GREAT FORM IS WITHOUT SHAPE

All life long
you are unhanding,
unhanding and unhanding
what was handed you.

All life long
you throw out the line of life.
You throw out the line, stinging
up from your guts.

Were they planting trees,
your father and your mother?
Did they ever plant?
Is that a line of trees
far away
green line?

All life long
you include something
that includes your life.
You are in the egg.

                (In the center of a picture,
          two angels hold a transparent crystal
          egg of teardrop shape. In the egg
          the ocean god is throned, left leg
          crossed over right, trident in right
          hand. Under his outstretched arms two
          children or little people stand, a boy
          at his right, a girl at his left. The
          boy's head is crowned with a sun, the
          girl's, with a crescent moon.

                    That's the middle level of
                the picture. At the top a blazing
                sun with human features dominates the
                vertical axis. At the bottom a man
                and a woman kneel on either side a
                furnace, man to the right of the
                furnace, woman to the left. In the
                furnace itself, directly below the egg
                containing the god, is suspended a
                similar egg, empty.   )

All life long
the dew falls from heaven
all life long
trees climb up from underground waters.

In the seed of the old god the new gods are swarming.

Earth is ready for planting.

The shut eye is opening.

The heat.

STEPHEN PHILLIPS AND THE WARMTH OF SUMMER NIGHTS

for my mother

   Ma donna, this music rode to harbor in a *blue deep hour*
& under a bridge of tears.

1. *…the darkness that we feel is green* my mother used to say to me,
    first time maybe by the Gates Mills unused polo field behind
      the stables
    and then she asked if I liked "poetry."
    I blew my nose. I didn't know the Word.

    So to Stephen Phillips, poet of *secret dawn*
    I owe confusion of my mother with Marpessa
    as well as early appellation of the Orphic gates.
    "In the Beginning," in illo tempore, the Word.

2. *the priest of bloom* climbed higher in the oranges of shaken nights
and Stephen Phillips, now hardly named,
bowed backwards down the boulevards of Gates Mills memories
with lost shouting ecstasies in a ring of stones beyond the
Beaumont's house
and the day "we" found a horse's skull far off in snowy woods.
Rough portage round the chagrin falls.
I went on planting pine trees. Summer nights
the mists were Chinese thick on Savage Road.

3. Stephen Phillips wrote, *how strange the summer night,*
   and truly summer nights are stranger than our mothers,
   stranger even than the ruddy fantasies we show ourselves
      sometimes before the fall of sleep.
   It is a broody hen, warmth and erethisia of a summer night,
   sweet camouflage of death and bushy mother of the world,
   thrust and consummation of the tiger's spring and orange
      presages of fall.

4. Now from *greenly silent and cool-growing night*
   Stephen Phillips' lulling mode returns to lap the ear
   in canticle of *wandering garden bliss:*

       Life is a flower
                                       My woe
       we crush between
                                         my early light
       so sweetness comes and comes
                                       my music dying

(This song for Idas of the greenest isle: *to me indeed,
hath a sea-rumour through the night been borne*   )

5. Our Lady of *mere felicity above the world*
   refrain your wintry blessing from the heights.
   Your idiom is ended, and your abstract love.

   Our Lady of *the unforgiven of this world*
   forgive us out of darkness and the warmth of summer nights
   and let our benedictions echo in the body's cave.

6. Marpessa chose a man before the God, chose
   odours of the open field and merely human intercourse.
   That summer Gates Mills afternoon when I heard the unfamiliar
       Name
   I blindly chose (was chosen for) the labyrinthine feeling way
   missing forever the plausible single track that leads to
       sanctity or successful office building home.
   My veins were green when Marpessa turned me on the Word,
   the sting, the wonder, not to be foregone,
   a training in, and of,
   warmth of summer nights, foxfire,
   under occult constellation Lioness.

   The labor is to wrestle with the Lioness
   descend to man with Lion Power firmly in the left hand held,
   that neither gods nor offerings pertain.

   Mother of Alice, Charles, and Gerrit,
   the tetrachord your Stephen Phillips sang is now antique
       and strange and under sea,
   but nourishing to men still is *the darkness that we feel is green.*

All italicized phrases are quotations from Stephen Phillips' "Marpessa," a poem whose virtue I would recall.

THE GREEN BOTTLE

The twelve Powers change in our bodies' changes.

My father, do you understand your son?

Now they weaken and withdraw,
now they drink of power and awaken.

My father, do you understand your son?

(He carries a boat in his head,
he has built it with his hands.)

I will not build apologies.
My strong ancestors are walking in the autumn air I breathe for them.
You have reason to be proud.

But do I believe it?

From the green bottle it is not wisdom I have drunk,
not joy, not strength.

It is remorse.

My father, do you understand your son?

A RED GHAZEL FOR C.B.L.
on his passage to India
(1963

The color red invigorates the traveller so to you I bring the
    red gazelle this poem
to wish you energy and health in India where eagle energy is taking you

and energy and health in England Scotland Germany and France
and on the currents of sustaining air along the continents.

It is a red gazelle that stands before you. There are blue gazelles
    with mournful eyes
(e.g. your running memory of boyhood lost blue mountain Colorado
    streams)

but it is a red gazelle that dances for you in these lines.
Poems come in many packages, like finance, music, engineering, prayers,

and though our mounts are not the same it is a poem in which you
    ride to India
as is this red ghazel from Persia Gerrit brings to you.

FROM UNDER THE MAT WHERE SAT THE CAT

Extricate, but not too much,
unfaithful digger of concordances,
let be the whole tasty clutch of it, rhyme
of I'm, not, awake,
child,
bequeathing willow trees beside a stream.
Not only old ravines
but Euclid Avenue,
my first escalator (Hal-ease Department Store)
were woven in the mat where sat the cat.
I say Department, was a sexual store
because Mother's store it was, her bailiwick,
father absent in a void called "Work."
Precarious. Don't try get it all in. Bailey's
was another tasty store, such glitterglass.
And later learned that testicles was store,
alaya-vijnana.
O dark dirty Cleveland, the Viking Club, the mysteries!
All I want is loving you and blank-blank blank-blank blank-blank.
It's only unmentionable because there's no end to chasing it
the tale of it and you and sustenance.
Hundreds are fleeing, but not hurricanes.
Violets, I always brought her wild violets in spring.
Breathless romanzas secret in the Flats.
Percolate the spiderwebs.
Not what you expected, eh?
I could bite you back, you furry thing, but you'd never understand.

THE MILK OF THE STARS FROM HER PAPS

1.   *in winter her body still nourishes me*

   out of the north
   feeding on berries, seeds of
     weeds rising above the long snowfields

     frozen apples in pastures, hayseed
  dropped in the barnyard where cattle are foddered

    maple buds, berries of cedar,

   out of the north
      feeding on catkins
        feeding on berries :
  the pine grosbeaks come
  the snow buntings come
  the pine siskins come

I come to her portals. The music resounds.

2.

      in the Horror Faces of the body, places,
      palaces,
      one cannot walk invisible,
      is known to thrones and dominoes, nomarchs of the mirror,
      hot shells pondering the passages.

      Through blue rock veins coarse messages of pleasure run
      as early rhymes return.

                              Kali listening.

Rainbow black me children's bodies in the senses of their mothers
who bear and bear themselves and shimmer in the forest,

Five footprints of the Camel, Miami doom voice
phones to tell me at eighteen I should have been where I now am.

Home, and Am, and Om.

                In other days

      Innocence availed itself of sweet confusion
      as jewels poured the light about her neck,
      morning finery.

Home is where she is who makes the sun bedeck the day,
love that leads all fear away.

           Don't get over it,
                 nor should,
rhythms like of natural orders that do exist as we develop us

            childhood sharps and flats
            returning to the natural,
                        key

              as if analogy were so.

Kali dances but what matters is that we can wear her necklaces
without real blame, because the blame is somewhere else,
in the midden, down there, behind the pleasure dome.

                              Day evens into Mahler's sleep
                              and we are made anew….

                ———

      From Mahler to Mozart is forward fast
on the wheel of the invisible old Public Gardens flower clock
where She stands beside me as I remember sailors
uttering benison night words of long black hair,
utterance of love,
                that earthly happenings be not forgot in water dreams.

      so springtime was a crop,
           manly flowers rising blue
     and I came in from Cambridge
              meaning to come beside myself:

     paratactic troopers' revelry the days we were!

     O Fortuna,
        we honor the dying by odors of confusion,
        profusion of our clement colors,
        as never they forgive unless we do.

These words are scarves of being we wind about our necks,
comforts
when the winter comes
as snowy night not lacking excitement.

What is meant is maybe tricky,

                tricks of youth who honor Kali,

   in the garden, under bridges

         pulsing in our happy palms,

tricks delicious to the mother as she sees the boys go down

and finally comes the untricked god who gives what we could only
  have forever

because his theft was only trickery.

Kali goes on dancing on recumbent Mercury.

3.
the theme of time is theft
                              city of loss
   Gloucester ravaged by selfish procuring
                        of the nature of the city itself
   fishiness of where we're at,
   so proliferates, it does, the disastrous abundance
   Armoricans wring from the sea and the shallows of Dogtown,
   the goddess' long body or barrow.
        Sweet, wine of such provender,
                                      and heady

to drink from the cup where she lays it heavy upon us,
our tongues in the glades of her heat.

      Not to be vilified
          ever "To Me, To Me" she sighs on whatever occasion.

      The sweetness of men is also her bounty
the milk of the stars from her paps runs sweet in their first jaculations
          in automobile cowboy privacy of nights in Dogtown
        where the sweet smell of clethra
                along the woodlots road

fills the moonlit air where her nectar falls on the fires of spring
and the gusher of spirit exults.

4.
    et la lune descend toujours sur le temple qui fût

    when barbarous and coldly bright and viper's bugloss blue
    you lay beneath the groined vault
    and read your image in my eyes,
    enactment of a memory that was still desire,
    did you contrive an issue which was out of time as out of mind?
    No specious legacy
    but happy change of mutual inductances or charge,
    veritable variocouplers in the kitchen of concomitance,
    the feeling you below me, and of It and THAT as good and
        strong as any holy book makes out
    Udgita. It was out,
    a moon that lay washed up upon our virgin beach,
    belonged to us
    white and perfect in its double usufruct and reference,
    a model,
    a clarity of style.

    Hands and legends do not fail
In the haunted temple the snakes below the ground were still;
beau clair de lune;
tops of radiance enjoyed themselves on cup and lance.
    Came alive, the classic scene:
    the dromena were carried round,
    exhibited,
    exsultet domine.

5.

        anádinidhana
        with large eyes moving slowly
        face smile-shining
        daughter of saffron and fame and brightness enfolding
        firmly established
        of lotus earth pericarp
        the cow is speech
        purely sustaining
        she-entering-the-cave
        abiding in song
          lalitámbika
           anádi
                nidhana

•

THE GLORY OF CHANGES

Father, good builder, favor this hymn
Rising in the changes it supposes,
Old colonists, fierce constant financiers,
Lean earthward in your sleep and bless the drifting young.

I.

For up and down America the young are drifting.
Their wild eyes suck up the power plants,
Feet beat a continent to poems.
Their dream, of discontent, enflames the fountains of the blood,
Their dream, of rapture, pulses in the sky.
They print emergencies on all the sensitive
And hail in goldenrod and apple blood that double dream
That never from the East came twisting
But shook one sullen boy spelled green
Against the buckeye black with autumn storm
Until his loins spilled this heavy raving cloud
That rides hard above the spurting villages and philadelphias
In the belly of the angry night of wands and water
To tongue our brazen colonies to celebrate
The thrust of novelty they symbolize.

II. *Your Version of their Discontent: Departure, Disgust, Despair*

You left Ohio for New York.
The flaming laundries gushed at your approach.
White horses thundered in the libraries,
Gods pitchforked heat from every stone.

Then you classified the bronxes,
New terminals disposed to brutal children.

But blood roars down the spinal gutters
As days hammer to a far interior.
On 42nd Street a dead man organizes vampires.
"Sleep is not available," the vegetables are drilling in your skull.

The cheap manuscript of night unrolls
And you reel on the rolling bed
Hearing always the gypsy girl crying in the tenements.
Will her passion never satisfy the immigrants?

The streets ache with nervous light.
The early papers say financial wizards block Venus in her transits.

You munch the crusts of dawn and jerk out sleep.
"The unemployed develop wings," the comic strips ejaculate,
And "The eclipse of youth is hourly expected."

III. *A Vision of the Wild Ones*

In a pasture by the sea the savage moon
Burns gold and golden green the famous torsos of the cyclists.
Gutted flowers quiver under black machines.
Their campfire is dead and sleep has spoken many.
They round the circle of an owl's eye,
Sad dissolving riders,
Shifting down the ragged sides of dream
Till water takes them in her final mouth.
These metaphysicians know no leader,
But one proclaims, rising on his elbow in the cup of silence,
"The red-caped Beast will tower from the mount of snows and trumpet
    Liberty and Love."

IV. *Your Version of their Raptures: Rejoicing in Discovery of the Doctrine of the Void*

That vision breaks the urban eye and flings aloft a burning gull.
"Love is the will to change, and change the will to love,"
The Statue of Liberty whispers. "Love is the law, love under will;
Not sleep, but voyages!" the sailor sings.
The shifting planes of solitude relax their vigilance
And thus the hot calamity of time dissolves.

You leap to California and the Western gate.
Somewhere in the secret hills an ancient grave is slowly giving birth
While images of beasts carol and adore.

Embarcadero. Your room is white and meaningful.
You drink black coffee to the sun which glitters under ground.
Sweet smoke fills the mounting room.
As the goddess bends you take and give,
Your body thrives in festivals of grape and honey
And joy trapezes in its animals.
Mind and mindlessness are one.

V.

Cameradoes, isolatoes, living in a change,
In a change foreseen gay like morning clouds
Crossing golden fields and purple forests,
Loving in a change, a change of solitude for solitude
Played in gardens haunted by an eagle's shadow and the rustle of a snake,

Moving in a change of time for time,
How deep and orient your glare
How purified your carelessness!

Love emerges from the filth of love:
Girls strike matches in the buried kitchens of their mothers;
Boys in bed machine the book of wheat until it sings to fly.

On the autumn mountains an old man muses, glorious and calm.
He blesses the origin of time and the drifting children of America:
"Love turns the leaves to fall and they falling turn the air to colored air."
All changes fall upon his upturned face.

III.

EXPLORERS

AN INLET OF REALITY, OR SOUL

(in this Age, or any

"With respect to plants as animals, we are wrong in speaking as if the object of life were only the bequeathing of itself. The flower is the end and proper object of the seeds, not the seed of the flower."
—John Ruskin, *The Queen of the Air*

When in Rome do as the Greeks,
show it hard,
let intellect be rampant in the flagrant colors of the indomitably so,
no compromise   no blame.
Take happiness in touch that bursts in light,
konx om pax,
as the sun yacht shoots through the Gate of the Tongue
(Tharmas happy in his element).
Sweetness savors itself in balling rondures,
delectation of the Gods come true,
truly come in the core of time,
old nick of it, new aeon, lion form in the wood where virgin lay.

When then love takes you in hand you don't languish in the clover
but make song:

>   o flowering stick
>   smoke wreath of peacefulness
>   discovery of happy self in other's grace
>   good limpid star   golden bird
>   girl leaning from a window when the last light shakes out in
>   the West.

This and *this* we say and do
and so we fix each other up and *this* is how transcendence is.

CLEAVING MAKING ROCK

Autumns and sunless afternoons
Shudder of birds in an empty sky:

      make make make make make

Whistling on the beaches
The shattering wind makes and makes

Who cleaves by storm is cleaving now
The ranging stones are cleft with light
And light deranges fuming words to flash and beat

Who is breaking in the holy waters?
Who is blacking out the last hard ignorant real thing?

The black wheel walks in the human heart
Rockets scream from seven gates
Bodies radiate new bodies, dissolve, eject themselves:
A raving mystery of birth, green award
And swash of buckling waters uncleaving,
Unleaving men like trees, unmaking cities

And mornings roll in from long surprises,
leave the beaches strewn with makings,
objects burnt by cleaving, but *here* and *now,*
by division made and black and subtle,
strong and dirty in a human beauty.
Their happy finders rock together naked in the sun.

Over the Western mountains
           golden petals fall in the Void
                  the pines are pines
            hermits listen to the waterfalls.
The Emperor drowses in the nature of the sun
A quiet butcher surely cleaves the royal bullock

HANDS THAT MELT LIKE SNOW

Do we hope much is that sentencing a river there in spring? Or isn't it the isn't it that answering is green?

Confusion is a gramercy where my sister clarity is singing. Let me ring that she says let me ring in the grass. It is us, it is ours, over us like watered silk or rock.

Silk and like is hoping through. Do we hope a grammayre equal to our hut? Or isn't well the lapidaire the well that answering is goodly bad?

So perfusion makes a speed that in our constancy stands up. Dressed in green, dressed in blue, figures lap their circles in the dark. Goodly bad or happily, a sentiment.

Ending now is licking like. Spring calls for swinging in the cool. A tilth, a milkmaid secretly. Her eyes, his eyes, the magnet so disposes, up and down. Holding fans at midnight.

TEA AT SLINKY'S PALAZZO

I sit in the tinted twilight of the Goonjaman

                thinking down the froward leaps,
       I am I in childhood clasp,
       to plangency of signifying stones
       dropped in secret well
       or well of secrets then.
    Huh,
sweet Ganja, softly run
as river of chagrin
floating genealogies
lapped in circumstantial mud of revery:

    "Here's mud in your eye," my father would say,
     Old Fashioned libation
     lifted in thoughtless whiskey rite,
     boyish fire sacrament.

Smoke floats in damask shade,
time purfled in this den.
What den now? Eyrie then or now?
Condensation. Purified.

       Another way to *hark the heart,*
       your heart the heart?
       Listening?

Scabrous notes recall the yellow cat,
the knowing cat, Slinky's cat wise in junky ways,
catwise by candlelight,
lavender echoes of a daft hello
turning in the drafty corridor
of a dingy "resident" hotel.

   "I've stroked a cat before"
       Marlene sang in some elsewhere dream or room
as fast to disappear as this,
and I am going out into the streets,
walk with the mob to Mammalapuram,
my father's route transposed behind my eyes.

I know Lady Audley's secret now,
"bride of God" indeed!

BRACKETING IN CITY THICKETS

Get your lovely bod out of bed you sleepy typewriter
you think this day is made for play it's
bright out, well it… Droopy streets await,
the puny are pining for that magnificence
we are clouds to bring them and
they'll never know hid in Jesus' pants
the winged prick they must caress or further deliquesce…

   ("I like to watch him get his gun" the sailor muttered
     as great angels rustled round us, looking down   )

Our heavenly host is called to mission of derangement,
inverted postures there the rule…

Grunt and please yourself there among the live ones,
 Lurk as you like, says the Book of the Law
  but never deride nor pity:
                       a grave joy behooves
as you flash the strobe tablets so fast they're never seen…

    Good misery   bad Gaiety
    fuck all night on Avenue Z

    but Bracketing-Down-the-Alphabet, they say,
    will get you a hit of heaven on Avenue A.

JUDGMENT OF THE CITY

I take
my length
in tarnished lights

dirty plate glass
cold friend
image.

Never
walked among
"the noble dead"
(who really has?)

Only know
upper B'way furnished rooms
naked bulbs

cigarette and cigarette
fingers calculating flesh:

"the noble living."

And still my eyes transpose
like tiger's eyes
this world's bloody meat
to everlasting bloody meat.

THE DARK GRAMMARIAN

His garret overhangs the green subtle slum
Where *nothing* culminates and, languorous,
The deathly adolescents play the dooms
Or flex their rubber summer nights to small
Experiments: *bent spoons snow gash hounds bright cock flame.*
His Book of Moons surrounds that life. Scholar,
Disdaining human love, he operates
The images of universal love
Until the blue-black circles fill with mist
And forms arise of jeopardy, crying
With wakeful eyes below the floor of speech.
His right hand takes the left-hand path, the Sign
Is born and flowers in the sudden damp.

Mournful angels spire down his black syntax
To health. Mad and warm as children, they splash
And couple in the joyous summer sea.

THE MALEFIC SURGEON

If death is what he seeks in life he fails.
Pale among marine accomplices
Or dark against the Arctic banks of sleep
He wields uncanny knives, small symbols
Of that wish to be transformed he must deride
Or bear the burning Mothers' cherishing
The child he is. Adoring crazy shapes
Of love acquits no night to charity
And never makes a face he has not cut
From desperation long before. Knowledge
Then is shrivelling, and he prefers cool
Averted gods who skill to father dreams.
Drifting in his watery nursery
Of brazen pomps, old nightmares stink romantic.

3 POEMS OF THE UNDERWORLD(S)

1.   *Black Currant Jelly*

Have you opened your head to the dead?
Do they puddle there, wire your voice box?

It comes in as he swallowed,

outside the door to his room the darker successions were waiting,

thumping and purring
thumping and purring.

    In the floor the crack opened
              and squeezing out gently
        on him it fastened.

He opened his mouth.

        Hard on this guerdon:
        to eat in order to sing.

2.   *A Birth in this World*

The scanners went rosy to feel him.
They sped to his eyes and extended their mandibles.

The zealots!

A banquet of sight!
Such stalks!
(such starry wind-walks!)

All use is abuse. The word of the Aeon.

3.   *Outside of McDonald's*

                  The prose of the dying,
                            who cares for that or this fall?

                  The riveting beauty

                        is a ketamine fountain,
                        the words to be found for,

as the-heads-of-the-gush-up-to-the-aethyrs

snort down through our forms to sustain us,

babble the obdurate poems, flash

our footing such rainbows.

3 ANECDOTES OF THE UNCANNY

1. *Seeing an Old One stepping out of a Saucer*

    "About nine feet tall. Yellow colored.

    Mouth like a bird, nose a high arch,

    bushy eyebrows five inches long,

    long ears, maybe seven inches long.

    On his forehead, three up-and-down wrinkles.

    Wearing something funny, a multicolored cloud."

2. *Night at Little Powder River*

"Sleep I could not; all so strange,

lovely, weird. White cotton trees,

the black river splashing slowly by, campfire's

strange gleams, in the distance

the mournful cry of the coyote, the shrill cry

of some nightbird, the swish of its wings -

a feeling not to be forgot. At last,

unable to keep still any longer, I got up,

walked noiselessly to the edge of the cotton tree clump

and looked over the wide expanse. My thoughts

flew home, what were they doing. How strange

if they could picture my whereabouts!

I was getting quite melancholy-romantic, when, ugh!

I suddenly stepped in some soft substance

that began to wriggle and squirm under my feet!

How fast I jumped back! I heard it scramble

off among the dead leaves and grass. I hurried back

to the firelight and my sleeping bag,

quite cured of any further wish

for moonlight rambles that fine night."

3.   *The Processors*

My buddy and I sat in a cave on Misty Mountain,

thinking about the Process.

A guy came up to us all dressed in yellow.

"Rest yourselves, weary Processors," he said.

We quickly looked into our mirrors.

There was a tiger!

>We said:

"Hey old tiger cat, belonging to this mountain,

how dare you pretend to be a man!"

The man changed to a tiger and soon departed.

PROSE FOR ST. CATHERINE'S DAY,
November 25, being the Marriage Day of the Wheel and the Cross

The Acts Reflections of the Acts. The Mirror nailed to the Cross.

"E's flat Ah's flat too," sang the Witness of Love, as the axe severed her cervical vertebrae. Her veins poured milk and sperm instead of blood and those who bathed therein were healed of their troubles.

Epousal our hope, and the mothering death with bandaged eyes confided to Catherine that she was being transported to the Bridegroom, as the Martyr had foreseen.

"But you're flying down, not up," she cried out, suddenly alarmed.

Death said: "True, Coins and Mirrors are nailed to the Cross (forgive us our debts but render unto Caesar and be thou perfect even). But the Irish Cross is contained in a Wheel. Hermanubis climbs up and Typhon falls down, Card #10 & turn it around. Ripeness is karmic and comic and possibly even phoneme of *k,* and we are bound for heaven still, though be it a cave under the hill, the sacrum is the skeleton of the Lord's Jonah-swallowing whale."

Catherine was silent with amazement, terror, delight: she thought she had broken for ever the Power of the Wheel, but was she now to awaken in the House of Light, a familiar in diamonds, another Wheel in her Bed?

IN THE GRIP OF THE OCTOPUS

To be useless is not without use,
as the temperature mounts,
and how we are offered the tincture of dog,
dementia unveiled in the niches where lions repose,
this burnt-out expanse.

Halidom, then, and she comes to your aid,
desire hard in the branches of icecream.

Veer, only to veer, a method of ease
      that is no method at all, a wash cloth.
Strip and proclaim, or whisper like hair of the wind
"No wonder the cowboy opens his fly
as the mother takes him in hand."

Eh bien, aujourd'hui, qui est l'émissaire du Dr. Wang Foo?

EXPLORERS

Coursing black savannahs, cruising broken cities,
the Explorer drew perceptive fevercharts,
slept with foxes, traded furs with wild children.
He learned to listen for the crackling of dry thorns,
beware the sucking mouths of slime that took so many,
and not to swim in haunts of moccasin and copperhead.
He was alone in his abandon and occasional rejoicing,
gave little mercy to his body as it bled away,
until by Northern quarries, on a littoral of seaghosts,
he found what he had never known,
the Companion, born-to-share,
fallow fellow in the ardors of the quest,
goer-with and polar traveller.
They have so many climates to explore, many seas to sail,
descents and climbs, vigils and expenditures,
reports to make of singing wires
and balances of wellhung crucibles
that it is a thing to praise, for them,
companionSHIP, companionship,
the pleasure of their company
and lighting up of loneliness
as each Alone is targeting Alone.

IV.

WORKING IN THE LOWER RED FIELD

WORKING IN THE LOWER RED FIELD

But handle the stone

free in the outburst
kindle a peace.

        Perfections are specialized. It is declared.

Do you want to shine
               softly
                          in the beam of forms?

But handle the stone.

        Wars only mirrors of the flame.
        Simplicity destroys reflection.
        White-robed kindred turn the air.

  As small as

  together in the bed,

    turning justice into their bodies
    making peace flow
    as sweetness affords it.

Birdsong in morning,
red sky at evening,
delights of the sailors,

but handle the stone.

PERIANTH

By far the best farmers

lovers are

whose bodies glisten in the light they make

and throw so carelessly around them in molten afternoons.

Husbandry

is what it takes to make the world splash in our heads

exploding water light

so nothing's unhinged,

the far fetched pleasure.

By fostering

the greenness comes again,

new arising,

flower world,

sweetness suck,

of naked verity.

    Afternoons are molten because melting is consequence of whatever passionate perception: without fusing them, the Flower-of-Mind makes all things capable of extremity, not adjectival, concentering,

as that toy lovers like us melt,

reform

in solar innovation,

our substances now justified anew,

made accurate by bliss,

a balance,

a tempering,

a style.

Perianth is the word I wrote

meaning the sepals and the petals

to remind me of the floral unity of love

and also how we double on ourselves the world

when our bodies shoot

and the heavens open:

how we suffice each other in ourselves.

ONE OF THE COMPANY OF LIGHT

The star man in my heart
is young and moves with all the strength
      memory masters,

shoots as a soldier in the boyhood game was
      supposed to,

 that brilliant and keen.
He is the might of the doom
    of the stalwart,
the heart of the men
    defending Maldune.
He is untarnished. He moves in the untold vigil
    of
      the children of others,
the warrior behind the dolor of actual war game stupidity.
Lucent he is, nothing lacking.
He is eminence fixed in the
    coldest blue eyes.
He is white, and renews the ancient *floraisons*.

Supple and amorous
he desires Christ and Achilles be one,

   and in the golden fields he sees them
      drink from one cup,

naked and hot in the heat of the sun.

THE CASTLE OF FLOWERING BIRDS

Fancy in the mind
The graceful flaunters of the summer air
Arise like flowers from their sea,
Bodies bronze and fledged in blue,
Uniforms that music wears
When most she is herself, not sound
Only, but fugitive and sly,
The fox occult among the grapes,
Anonymous in summer's horn.

Brilliant beyond a self, the birds
Are dumb with feeling, an afternoon
Of wings. The company of love,
Safe in the garden that is themselves,
More ghost than garden, more brute than bird,
Acclaim the throbbing animal,
The beastly petals green with blood.

TO WEE VIRGINS TO MAKE MUCH OF TIME

Photo the wreck

before it spaces away.

Flash is what you got

to make it fast

as bash is behovely

and beauty is swash

and swags in the wind.

MAKES THE MIND GROW DULLER

        To you the way is thru myself.
        I labor in the knowledge of difficult estrangement
        when what I am with is most away
(this is like-Elizabethan wisdom I never could have guessed was really so:
  all those felonies of antique poesy and all).

        So I am myself a little absent-minded,
        that's minded of absence, and c'est moi.

WILD CHERRIES

I remember how

calm as bodhisattva head

and as music blissfully

you slept my love

in my faithless-faithful arms.

THE CONDITIONED

Absence of accustomed love is death.

O I remember unaccustomed

                                          days!

A FEBRUARY MIND HUNG UNTIMELY
UP IN SUMMER'S WEAVE

    Voyager far away,
dreaming of snow in florid day,
what though your brumal mind outrun
        fat brimming sun,
anatomize cold time and slow;
      to *now* unkind
   still summer words you find
wriggling below the speech you know.

   The tropic god decrees
a brogue of summer destinies.
So what, that winter antedate
       unwelcomed fate,
from being *now* you can't forbear;
     so speak in haste
   the hot love verbs at last,
good banyan shadow you from fear.

(end rimes & scheme after Thomas Stanley, 1647)

A GHAZEL OF ABSENCE

(blue Ghazel, for D.

If I had trained a gull I'd send it off to Boothbay Harbor
(like Solomon to Sheba, like Hafiz to his Friend)

bearing greetings & compleyntes of absence
from "the cypress envying your figure & the moon bowled over by
    your face."

The bird would say: *   you there, captain,*
though you are Absconditus my heart is touching you

sunrise to sunset the winds weave endlessly between us
& let of my Affection the boiling deepsea currents testify.

Lest the warriors of grief ravage your beauty (la Beauté)
I send you the ransom of my self-love, keep it,

musicians will play out Gerrit's desire
in the mode of this poem which is like a "gazelle."

I SEE BRIGHT SUN ILLUMINATING ABSENCE

snow on juniper

to the feeding station flies

for bread no red bird

SONG: *L'Amour est echoué*

"Love sits on coral reef, himself
Of coral formed and delicate,
White and red like a summer cloud
At sunset heeded, faintly blue
And exquisite in all that pomp
Slowly sinking with the shipwreck of the sun."

This song I heard uncertainly.
These images, lonelier
Than eye can dream of silences,
Addressed the future as the past
With noise of flutes and corybants,
Figured out in other words
The sullen bases of our certainty.

THINKING OF THE EYEBROWS OF MY LORD

Into radiance

                              sunt lumina

        it comes upon me,

                beside a lake,

      not yesterday's elation

but shattering that is wonder.

           Express the grape

                        the angel said

       exhaust yourself

         and so the stain uniquely gives consent

                    you may be loved

that of all uneasy things

you come to drink of it,

Islam,   submission to His Kiss.

ALBA

"That was the clock
 I have to go."

"Twenty minutes more in bed,
 My body's warm, the air is cool."

"I've got to be at work by nine."

"I kiss your legendary throat,
 When love's at work the world is sunk beneath the sea.

 Press your body onto me.
 See,
 We flow together like molten gold and molten gold."

THE RECLUSE (fragment)

Is it so bad to be forlorn

wandering daisy fields

harking to a faroff horn

eating honey music yields

AMPHION
& his song

AMPHION.

        Darkness climbs the afternoon diamond
        long and lazy in which he lay
        hearing the golden earth body hum beneath him.
        Grassy dream of summer of green grass.

        Open to darkness, open to light, a muse
        in the shifting, a shape in the hands of the winds
        that cross on the headlands of antic ridings,
        his Will elects building a song, a city
        to elevate, go down, in his acceptance of season:

his song.

                Here are the towers

                Here are the flowers

                Flowers of the city of earth

                These are the avenues

                For strangers exchangers

                This is good news of the city of earth

                Here are the tenements

                Yet green in their cerements

                These are the gay movements, benedict

                Music of the city of earth

                City of earth

BOXCAR MOONLIGHT SCENE

Furtively, then freely

they made it in an empty boxcar

moonlight streaming in the open door,

two o'clock in the morning,

relaxing,

each eager for the other's pleasure,

faster and faster,

mouth to body fastened,

enjoyment like forever and then at the same time time shot off into eternity's gullet.

Stars strung out like mistletoe over a heavy sky,

peace, the necessary return to normal economy, being

what each one was and is, kisses of satisfied friendship.

A COMFORT IN THE LONGING FLAMES

Of rock,   time and landforms,
   perfervid utterance of love:
the black man pours it out
my love for you,
                              cock stars dawn trill
incontinent as bull clang power shout.

Comfrey,
              a handsome plant,
containing allantoin cell proliferant,
very difficult to rid the garden of,
knits the bones and soothes the hurt of not to be with you,
until I can see you attired in your body glory robe,
glowing sun lamb prop of heart and willing mind.

LOVE POEM

The purport not to be silenced

      is color of love,
languishing bodies striving to be, explode in sweet asters,
turning all unfulfilled meaning to glory, an ark.

    Here we parade, all animals, us,
    as our hands create each other's appearance,
    flashes of lilac, of gold, of apple, of sunset,
    eyeballs, accoutrements

            whereof speaks bliss

      This remember of me,
      just that I loved you,
      just camera, jury my love.

HOW WE SIZZLED IN THE PASTURE

         for Kenward Elmslie

Down in the boondocks rhematic sinsigns multiply

    jug jug to hungry ghosts,
     busting open pearly gates.

"Aint no grace, aint no guilt,
  popcorn twiddle, come full tilt"

    handy pathfinders whoop

       at no-restriction hurdles :

  Da woid ob sin aint dare at all,
   not in giggles nor reddening toes

    no think blink
    no tattle no buckle
   high dick fun at the fair.

Vestigial legisigns just don't operate,

healthy wisps entwining and buzzing,

hinterland busy with fresh huggermugger.

     Replica points:
    you point your toes
   in fact it's toes we fluffily toss.

Secret moon lotion rub by reedy pool.

"They call me Googoo" I said, I.....

                        All upsurge, hot tip
                        green informants signify
                        the trees are barking
                        "cheeze it, the cops."
                        Trees tease, twinkle.

That need of being versed in country things:

                            guiltless I milked the cow,
                            slaughtered chicken,
                            swam with snakes,

unjust barefoot hobbledehoy

                                            ahoy.

THE JOINT IS JUMPING

Whose joint? Pass me one, please,
et suçe ma bite. What's the time?
Across the great divide the caravans tick,
and tremulous, we unlocked our hearts,
lips on lips, AHA the stars were bright
as fell the fullness we fall into, not two not won,
a foretaste, cool hole of in-between, pleroma.

We lop the moon, invoking hazard's sorites
our sorties through the orient gates.
Tumulus, the earthly place of such angelic music,
is lively now, jumps, is locus where we slither out of time.

MELANTHUS IN THE MOUNTAINS

The night is warm he walks the mountain road,
Midsummer vapors veil the Hyades.
His shepherd's pipe is sharp to mock the toad
Shooting unruly songs from dripping trees.
But the equal contest bores him soon,
He rubs his amber flanks with dew to take
Another dare and wrestle with the moon
Who dazzles naked in a mountain lake.

Alone and sensual, he figures love
As combat, dreams the maidens' votive dance
Incites the satyrs from the holy grove
To spring to them and rip them out of trance
Until, by terror warmed, and dark with mirth
And doom, the shudd'ring couples sink to earth.

(Youthful homage to Stefan George)

ROMANZA

They were at their restaurant. They had finished their coffee and everything else too, although they couldn't know that because they were very young. They were one and another.

One was saying:

…"then I looked up into the bright sky that dazzled like a Blue Sahara, emptied of all furniture but the lust of emptiness and one silver airplane, another fish entirely. The airplane engraved a circle on the air and I was afraid of circles. But the airplane dropped toward me and became a soothing bird, a vulture with the head of a Saint Bernard. Its wings beat up the air from Ischia intemperate and palmed my eyes with dust. It was almost on me when from its kindly leering jaws fell an enormous silver key-ring with one tiny silver key attached. This key-ring was the burden the bird was born to bear. But I was glad because I knew that this was the key to the Giant's Tomb on the marble cliffs and I lifted up the ring in spite of a double fear, for I knew that the queen of circles is the queen of tombs.

"So, bowed under the weight of the enormous silver key-ring which I carried on my back I climbed the miles of slippery marble cliffs. The Giant's Tomb was the largest of all, but the tiny silver key turned easily in the massive lock and the portals of the Tomb swung open. I passed in, through a landscape dizzy with ferris-wheels and the summer cries of children, to the central washroom which is the sanctum of the Giant's Tomb. Outside the washroom door an old Spanish lady was rocking in her chair with such madness that her motion nearly described a circle. She was knitting a black turtle-neck sweater which she had almost completed, but her knitting-needles were so enormous and unwieldy, the propellers of an airplane, that they kept turning in her hands and falling off her lap onto the floor. I guessed she might be the queen of tombs incognito, but since I was only a knave I didn't attempt to penetrate her disguise with my style, which is rather ingenuous anyway.

"In the washroom a portable phonograph gave off an endless gay waltz. It hung in the air like the incredible face of Rachmaninoff. The washroom attendant, a grand black broth of a boy with the powerful body of a thirteen-year-old boxer, was engaged in slaughtering calves. He was quick about it but careful and scientific. Over the urinal holding the stupid staring faces he deftly slit each distended velvety throat with an old-fashioned razor. The moony face of the urinal was clouded by red-hot anger. I was overcome by such passion. On all fours I pranced up to Our Saviour, softly bleated, and extended my throat to His ready fingers. But alas! the sensitive youth, distinguishing, rejected me, and, drying his hands, offered me on a white towel a brush, a comb, a nailbrush."

The tale was finished and they had finished too and now they knew. The other looked steadily at the one and said, " 'Enough or too much.' You must agree that under these conditions marriage is impossible." And separately they left the restaurant. They were through.

HISTORY

It is a revolver like love
But more dignified; a foreign affair;
The wide-eyed lady lying in wait;
The asylum looking so like a garden
It fairly takes you in.
It is the fanciest hotel,
Delicatessen and sumptuous source,
Appointed with parks and pianos, pleasures
Endowed with appropriate vistas,
Fresh exhibitions in all the rooms,
And such far-fetched flambeaux. At night
Each guest discovers in bed a boon,
A real surprise package, a promise
Brightly wreathed like a dream-boat…

But in the dark beneath your pillow
Something lives and moves and has its being.

It's awkward to open the package,
Glimpse an unsuitable nightmare,
At your shoulder the dear smiling giver.
What you can't expect from the past
Are the trappings of the spring,
Gowns to wear at the sun's reception
Or to meet the filmy negligence of rain…
One might wish for other hands,
For opalescent crosses,
For a creamier solution,
But not for this…

In the casino the black *chanteuse*:

*'Le plaisir passe
Il me dépasse…'*

NEEDFIRE

Impure
of necessity
I cannot shut it out
the poem of fire
that burns in the night
men know not how to use.
A way of love,
lines of flame
too familiar
to be a god.

It is the keyboard of desire.

GOING GREEN IN THE FALL

      into darkness, gone. *A l'envers de son noir.*
      What hides is what bides.
          I'm in a cloud not bad but red.
      Say the lake was yellow with yellowing leaves,
      The light was gold and bold to our eyes.
      So bold we told each other our untold love.
      Being smitten it's called.
          Lift, only lift, your upsidedown head.
"Boo" said the bird of unlikely color
 as I move in your body
 and rain will fall again and again
 and night folds day in its lava hands.

THE UNSEALING

Born to presence in bornlessness
                born to be wild
                    to be wildered
       having not but knot unraveling
            revealing namelessness
to poverty we can climb in this unsealing.
       A tree, an oke, a Krystmesse oke,
unseals itself to spring,
                the shape is never still,
a fragment of a fragment of…

and down some garden path you walk,
may hop, in hapless May,
as odors of the spring unseal themselves
and who is indiscernible not hesitates and in that destitution is
                    the freedom of a spring,
                    a mode that not returns.

With all this minding, we kiss,
        fullness springs to hand   ripe to come
               and sun abounds.
                    Marvelous liquefaction!

V.

A PLACE

PLANTING THE AMPLITUDES

Of sea-stoned altitudes the constellated swing
                            salts my gloried eyes, makes free.

              I am here as I am here.

"Finding form" one calls this opening or sunburst

 not "the tolling of the sea"
 or other cantilene.
                        Time is not the sea not like the sea.

Disposal of you trash of memory,
        have gone / "made in Europe"
        analogies that fake the line
        like "heirlooms" / family ideas.

I hold the stick of bareness
to be hard man wilding exquisite
                                    and bateleur.

It is of course not simple place this seeding
of COURSE / like water course / a moving water meeting
            (in Gloucester Heraclitus yes)

but I know for every man
there are places, amplitudes
signatures of heart
he can plant and he must plant.

BLUE DECREPIT TOWN

It takes me, here I am, living in a place I first drove through twenty
   years ago,

teaching John to drive,
(me who was no natural American boy driver,
though learned it driving tractor)

driving through,
then,
nervous
about these real narrow streets of this decrepit town

nervous
about all the cute rough boys
standing
in front of three pool halls

nervous
about the kind of life to lead when no more college

nervous
about even what to do in bed and with whom,   as the limerick goes.

Now it appears
                        that driving through this place
looking mostly straight ahead but glancing at faces and bodies and
   decrepit dirty buildings

     was more than it was, then,
                            just driving through a different place,
teaching John to drive,

nervous,
thinking of sex,
thinking of the ocean which everywhere shone through that autumn day
    because I had never seen the ocean to make it with before, being
        just a heartland-America boy.

Now it appears
                that what gives us a shove
                              even to love,
     the pattern we are hung up on
                            or where we fell off
arises
        like the character of a golden lion
                            purely through causes,
    flickering lights of a decrepit town,

is as empty as causes,

and may be grabbed by the throat of mind

much later, if at all, if you're lucky, if you've lived well,

when you're no longer nervous, or differently nervous,

not only
        in seeing the whole jewel-net flicker in the depths of the sea

but even
       as song flickers
                    in the sight of

                        blue decrepit reality town

                                    wherein dwells Love.

HONEY FROM THE ROCK

My love must hold to fluency
as to statute, fable,
rock of what imprints us in the shakes of being where we are.

Hold
to the shifts of light
hold
to the spring and heap of water brings it in, junk
of night and flowers, takes it out.
Sweet flag of dawn,
our integrities are all the inroads we can make,
their poles.

Life sucks itself to life in Granny Day's swamp
as I wait for you
and you for me,
and bullfrog music environs common spring.

Rain fills the pools,

I cannot declare my love
but
it holds to fluency as I imagine holding you.

NEW COMMENTARY ON AN OLD TUNE

"My love must hold to fluency"
  and you must hold
  to the poet loving you
  with fluency
  your love must hold to fluency
  as the great tides of day and night give ordonnance,
  measure,
  to the lines I throw you from my heart.

Heartlines intersect between the stars.
The stars are in the rock
and cattle drink from the swamp miscalled of Granny Day.
(No appellation equals that-which-cannot-be-fixed.
An appellation falls from the tree. It is good to eat.)

It is a rock of dawn.

And jubilee to love,
may be quiet jubilee or noisy jubilee,
but always jubilee, this oyster, this apple.

Fluent,
the round
from
sediments
through magmatic action to
the granites
through meteoric action
to again
sediments,
the round of water, fire, earth, and air.

Such a fluent rondo is love.
Do not fear my love of others
so I care for you.
"Every man and every woman is a Star,"
and stars are in the rock.

There is no war between the stars.
They are perfected or perfect themselves.
To be loved, in their integrities,
each one for himself. Love my love, my apple.

So let your love flow and fall from heaven
to melt the snow beneath
and in our throats the bursting song and
we will come together again,
and bullfrog music shall environ common spring.

DUSKY

                    filled with

   (by plasmatour)
                                        rain

        grey syllables

            Goose Cove

                    Reservoir.

SUNSET AS EARLY WARNING SYSTEM

Inordinately extending

vision wraps surpassing up.

The harbor and the gulls this picture,

and all virgins elevated to the last clenches of light.

How many? I do not ask, it is the instant of convergence, the flare.

And so comes in me as hymn the world

and unfigured spin of dimensional being

beyond anecdote, well, undesignated,

apt to make of Gloucester roofs a diagram.

ABBADIA MARE

in memoriam John Hays Hammond Jr.,
April 13, 1888 – February 12, 1965

                Like Tintagel, this Gothic camp
                      (*castrum, castellum*) is piled
                      on the rocks above a northern
                      sea. But here! in this Mass-
                      achusetts fishing town where
                      the loom of Europe fades!

On this invented house
Harangued and fabled by the sea
The emptiness of great night falls
And we mount the corkscrew stair,
Ignoring flagrant chasubles,
To greet the shabby moon
That tramples the waters to golden unrest.

Urban hells seem fictive here,
Where mind reflects the motions of the sea
And of the Gothic past. Time flickers
In the salty, star-pricked air
And the Gloucester buoys dip.

Yet even here is noise of death and blood
Gulls' jagged screams impale the night.
There, that blacker shape is Norman's Woe,
A reef made infamous by poetry.
Gulls nest there, rest from killing.
Rats swim out at night, Jack says, to feast,
Red eyes advancing through the waves,
A meal of feathers and of blood.
Downstairs again we talk of automatic death,
The hydrogen bomb and the Aquarian Age.

But we turn from the follies of human speech.
Thai the Siamese cat is asleep.
The ear is hallowed and taken by music
Mingling with the ocean's recurrent faith.

Here immured in fidgets of a faithful age
Faith! each one thinks, apart. Faith! Make faith!
O weak weak weak weak!
Good simplicity of water, rock, and brilliant moon, *you* are enough.

POSTCARD ON HENRY DAVID

Dear Charles,

    what no one says abt Thoreau
    is how he made it as a poet
    not in his poetry in his prose & life he soared

    his approach to Nature as he made it, capital
    was orgonomic   functional

    he was Psyche's early animist
    prophet of gestalt Mythology & Buddhist of attention

    what he missed we think we know
    but his gain made him Thoreau

                            Love,

                                  Gerrit

("Thoreau was not

    thorough"

        – Charles' comment on card   )

THE CURVE

    how one incurs
             the burden of a city
                        and Indians!

      this is where I came in

            by the pest-house, through the old woods
            (not over that flubbery span no sentinel owns

      comes into one's own,   reality

            making the place by pacing the place, live
            (or live,   change vowel eye,   heart

      the stature commensurate
      to the gist of the nation,
      imagination   . . . . .

against the curve, the way it slants in,

      the lay of the land
      unseen but by
                        Indians!   then
(thanks ever be to Charles Olson for "Indians!"   then

                                                  . . . . .

   the alien eyes, mine eyes have seen the,

 mine eyes alien
         Dutch
    not Indian!
           outer planetary,

  were keener for the curve,
  how wolves and lions came in
  ("some affirme that they have seene a Lyon
   at Cape Anne which is not above six leagues from Boston"

              . . . . .

so I round another man's measure to round out my own:

         to speak of "discovera"

 the pristine we work to inherit,

        native lode

           to shoot out again,

 is not to make up, Harry Martin,
        some queer hemisphaera,

 it is to smell
 to dig with the hand
 to demonstrate
     and at least

    to reclaim
    to come in

       like Indians!
           on this curve

  from the ravening wood

     to a city

     we once could be citizens of.

A SIMPLE FIRE OF WOOD

Love, too much likeness saps.
Lovers' difference sustains their love,
the stalwart sailor and the poet

I used to dream that sailors dreamed of other sailors
but now I guess it is of poets and hearths they also dream,
two cats before the fireplace.

Two cats before the fireplace.
In slanting light of ravens' wood
we decided for a rosy hearth
to keep the fire virgin in,
where the poet and the sailor,
happy criminals in love,
united in a rhythm simple as the poem,
two cats before the fireplace.

THE BOULDER BEHIND THE HOUSE
(after Li Shang-Yin)

    a thin rain from the East, a mist,

                over Mill River

  delicate thunder.

           Here be no gold toad of luck,

no tiger of jade,
          but in the back yard

              a red brown rock,

        grim Enceladus-immense,

  shoves out of the earth.

Once a great heiress, behind a screen hidden, loved with her eyes a handsome poor youth.

A river goddess rose once from the water to give a great prince her pillow of love.

Mere instances.

Will your heart gape
                        wide with spring flowers?

The candles of love fall into ashes.

The rock is auroral.

STROLLING PEBBLE BEACH IN FEBRUARY

    His rock is not my rock
    nor yours, hot your palm makes it glow,
    that core a whirlpool in the rock.

        Stoned, we listen, dumb,
        or see one red bird
        in a jungle of grapevines.
    This is looking at a lot of paintings in the sky
    but seeing one master scrawl.

        Underlies, it does, spread of choices
        Wamba's fan-shaped destiny,
    rocky patternings
          to find, to find,
                    refined
                            perception.

ANNISQUAM NIGHTS

I tell you it was real
bayberry bushes on the hill,
the house, yellow moon and simple love.
But o fox laughter from the woods
the white fox running thru the pines!

VI.

SOME GONE

A FAR MEMORY OF LAZY SPRING

if you are addressed "you are addressed"
but the composition is rain,
erases as it addresses
itself to the task
and it's early spring you are walking
not looking for work
"call me the tiger of boozy woods"
your laugh can only kindle her itches
and we knew it covertly, part of the action,
she lolling beside the burntout fountain
hers the sidelong glance so classic,
and faithless is as faithless does
as blithe as skipping to her side
and hand in hand
and who is drawing this fancy
out of the well of past caring
a long cool drink
while a friendly alien supplies warm liniment
to soothe the lineaments of loss

DEAD MAN BLUES

(To be uttered very slowly)

Do you know you energize me so
easy, no, being dead, to know,
ready or not I'm coming any way
(you're not dead you're hiding, no)
katabasis a way to go…

Despite fatigue and foliage fall
extends a grace of quietude
reclaims and constellates
your death to wring from me the wrongest cry,
kelson of transmembered diamond night.

Derivative of long song, this
everts a passion past
relief, some die expecting it, a death,
you did not, October morn so red,
knowing at lost last minute only last of life.

THE BEREFT

To be forgiven in the air of autumn by the born again

old voice meandering along the willows and in such antique music as she wore,

some night blue lady whose booze- and coke- racked bosom viol became Elizabethan legendary dark

deep song to wrench a memory

of love we treasure in the measure of pavans and city dumps.

I remember rose hips, a body writhing as it spent itself,

and now the change of sky, fading colors of hairy roses by the sea,

      salt spray against skin.

  It is sufficient suffering to vanish never,

trace new silhouettes of loves against that sodden esplanade of fall,

count the newly gone who move among the living and cry long
      animadversion in our sobs and indrawn breath.

  I think of Selma, Steve, and Charles.
  Names haunt midnight veins and Times Square daylight roar.
  John and Ruth, mercy, steadfastness.

  The wind is in our heads,

  no matter what we drink or pop into blood,

it shrieks across the blinded avenues and swathes our bodies in the
   filthy net of memory.

To be unforgiving is to live.
                            When we, bereft of love,
          realize to forgive ourselves and whom we love,
          we spend,
                    rejoice in good forgiveness of those we never loved
                         enough

               bereave ourselves at last in glory

                         and we die.

AMAZING GRACE AND A SALAD BOWL:

> in memory of Stephen Jonas

…And of the dead,
the dear gone new into the ancient halls,
                        "the melody lingers on"
—a favorite quote of his—
                        his melodies do.

    Is no repair on earth
    for broken nerves,
    wornout heads, the injuries the sensitives
                              self-inflict.
The god of this world treads on brains like grapes.
In the winepress what can we do but sing
                if we are men at all.

1.

                you are gone Esteban
    & yr big brown body just isn't there to hands you chose,
                    Hotel Madison men's room boys,
    weird high objects of yr unearthly love,
    dumb credit card thieves, boosters, drunks,
    the last junk of the world.
        They shift without you on the esplanade,
        and I shift without you, like yr other friends,
who have their own memories of yr kindness, cooking, talk,
                yr body that changed and changed.

2.

      I have a salad bowl,
      unpolished wood
         I cherish as of you best memory.
      The courtesy and purity of greens,
      lemon juice and olive oil.
      You wove a fabric beyond yr words,
      ideas I sometimes felt were crazy,
      a coat of hospitality,
      embracing wine and merriment,
      of Boston dawn, the place of time you loved.

3.

      Boston you were to me, after I left New York
       hub of, haven,
   Would pile in exhausted from nights of pleasure,
               to hear yr morning chatter,
  drink coffee, sometimes beer or wine.
You knew the Boston crevices, their histories, the rats,
                     and marketplace,
        how to get electric free,
         clothes, hi-fi parts, good affabilities.

4.

      '*Du musst dein Leben ändern*' Rilke wrote,
       & how poesy transforms we disputed oft,
      not denying that it does, it sure does.

Now, sunset fading, I wonder what the panoply of spring was worth to
   all of us,
the price of all that agony, the sky on fire.

   Boys moving through the blood, the witless loves,
the loved ejaculations and again and again the upturned wild faces.

For you, a reason found in madness, a cap on mere existence.

   You denied the ecstasy I claimed,
     said tricks were only tricks,
    which I in turn denied,
       but you and I together knew

     bright words hanging on the boughs of dawn.

        Amazing grace.

FURIOUSLY FRAMING, STEPHEN JONAS JAUNTILY

Socially available and yet without a horse. Transmogrified the youthful dancing (black) to exercise of mind and ear, perception of social determinants furiously framed and pivoted on bosky chant of street and market. Eerie sports impressed. Prevented by denial, no sweet tooth but political messages crackled out from it. Ho for apples from wistful farms of long desires, the prisoner's face at the bars. Entropy and city glare. Now "life in African societies seems, possibly even more than our own, to be marked by a discontinuity of experience in the encounters and status dramas of daily life."

Jovial, rage against the cheaply liberal, but love of juvenescent trackers. Off to a bad start, but never hopeless, furiously framing snow men from distant mountains lost in Boston gullies. Never seen the finest hand unbetrayed by nonsense. Always a version of benevolence. Sibilants begin and end prophetic rant, but gentlemanly demeanor still goes with rolling gait, call and response in Blackstone Park, and *the musician unifies his time with the last beat he plays,* so Steve with ease and as you please.

FOR JOHN WIENERS, 1934-2002

there, airy but steady...

    throughout his long life of downs and ups
John Wieners never wavered from responding
to a faroff calling   what remains
his poems fragments of a disordered devotion
always his primal leading, glimmer of dusk
and hits, blue, gay, and mad, fighting anxiety
in colored boxer shorts on lonely beds, snowlit
in inky storms, flash hotels with neon glow,
until exhausted
the sound of drums in early afternoon, the poems
echoing our marvelous faults, their fruits.

from THE ORCHARDS OF SLEEP

FIVE POEMS IN MEMORY OF ANNA KAVAN

THE CASCADE

 It vanishes. You have moved away. You become somebody to read about.
 A thin fame envelops your flounces, the flame has licked through your features. Retiring began in the room that composed you, your mother's tinkling enclosure. Way back you heard the sounded retreat, among the dancing boys and girls. You refused incorporation.
 Daisy face, they pointed. Preferring the willow, the rose, the cascade, you will vanish in the forgetting storm and be grateful.
 A gravity.

Of the sojourner or fleeing woman.

She heard the song of Israfel.

Without leading is no finding, that is being led. Though she hears the song of Israfel, unless she follows she is dead. Fear of death leads her dying, taking her to places without wedding.

I can't sing wedding, she trembling. But what I have is up to me, it is given, and there is the star.

The angel plucks unusual strings.

She was the Hanged Man swinging. Too old to be, in a tree, she feels, but she cannot deal with agelessness, the cards are blurs.

The guitar stings her awake.

UNSITUATED SLEEP

I am the princess of blurred sets, she says, and thereof the peculiar process.

Your morning bird soars above my towers, my catastrophes are roaring in your bed, as day is fended.

How specially concur reflected brilliances!

THE LIZARD'S EYE

The wall is full of lizards watching me.

Outside palm trees shake maddened by the torrents. Within, the torrents terribly echo. Or ache. What is this old castle no one knows?

For whom do I wait, wrapped in a cloak of invisibility? That stranger, just crossing the bar-room, so beautiful he must be, carrying flowers, death.

I am known to lizards' eyes, quick and indifferent, attending. And there are lizards behind the mirrors, here.

SUMMER'S EROSION

granite, burning with mineral fires…or such a wish of nowhere green I repudiate, but where is the eye to know so? An icicle of fire burnt before her, as she swayed slowly in the dark old rendezvous. To be erased, who is open enough to allow the eyes? Some one can, or some two or three or four or more. Four or more is moving blue and moving true, as he moved slowly blue toward her icicle of fire. Like a summer evening and its grace. And its going, going.

ELEGIAC FANTASY, DELAYED IN GLASS

in memory of David Rattray

Elegy is distance and thereby memory and whisper of the winter wind that sings between the darkness long mistaken for a light expanding like the water flower, and a morning redness mistaken for, sometime glad, extinction,

    brown sugar that melts from grim to wistful,

    will you rise to rampant red as peony, good doctor,

thereby, so by "thereby" absence enlarges to touch your body simplified all over everywhere in desire under and around, ground and variations of some love,

    and is warranted, warmest sooth, roses from the merry devil

and urged by urges new, needs to be explored in the service of, in not centered center, whose will or what directs we do not know, slow, being so and only so licensed to rovers, these tongues and hands,

    what explosions, lassitude, explosion, o lassitudo!

Extolling, thus, the gratitude and eerie recognition, afterwards the peace that promises the seed of still future glorious storms.

༄

A tempered doom lies on the rug like history, barring the flight to remorseless islands bathed in golden light where was offered immortal fruit. The given stuck. Surprise! The fool on the hill claimed I would recognize the foiling fatal speed of time when I reached his speed, but when did,

I scorned his sagesse because the force between our singularities, yours and mine, was independent of the separating speed.

That history, no crystalline delay, tempered what was called our frailty in those faroff days and nights we feared the forest.

ع

Though the archons assuage to mystify, swathe us in their mummy-clothes, such purposes only yet assuage False Will, False Mask, unrealized errant Husk, and Fate's fell Body,

>	and so by halt or exercise of stop we

>	preserve the purity of lust

>	unfailing light that played on puppet limbs

>	and in alembic danced.

Indistinct it is to elegize or laud, it is to swing,

>	foot the ancient round,

>	under crystal mutable.

>	Aha.

SKELETON ECHO

The clock that numbers me has told and tolled my history
but my story of invention is not done:

I am walking still in the golden sunlight of the midsummer mystery.

AUGUST DESOLATION PLY

Hot dawn
Desoxyn gone
mind forlorn
nothing born

hand weaves a lonely place to lie in.

AUGURIES IN AUTUMN

Cool leaf

        rides light down

one windrow

            nearby falling

apples beckon snow.

OCTOBER SONG

Who is rich in love will lay
An autumn table for his guest
And shape in autumn ornaments
The shapes and omens of his love
So from these purple frets his love
Will take for sure that when they lay
Away all summer ornaments
And evening is the normal guest
He will not be surprised. What guest
Would snub his friendly honest love
That laughs at foolish ornaments
And tumbles them in straw to lay
A guest in ornaments of love?

VII.

ON EARTH, PARTICULAR

WEED UDANA

Food is not the Enemy.

Certainly Food is not the Enemy.

For the third time, and now most and I make it most true, and to be held in the refrigerated water of flower of mind, Food is not the Enemy.

Only if Life is held to be the Enemy, can Food be so conceived, and that Life is the Enemy is a burning distraction, conceived by Life itself as part of its gag (but no one has to be muzzled).

And this not to say, that other boring half kernel long known, that *we* are the Enemy, because there is an Enemy, and it's no good pretending it's some hypothetical you or us.

Or a Weed.

What is a Weed? A dirty word to be abolished as we reinhabit Adam's old garden and softly or lovingly roughly caress the genitals of God and Goddess, walk in the beauty of morning and evening rubefaction forever. A weed is nowhere, or we are all weeds, all woad, all meant to be eaten, as I carelessly weeding one noon pulled up by mistake coriander, blessed it for food the next day (brown rice with *cilantro*).

So many friends to play with we have. Weeds are, what we smoke, we eat, we work with, what we are, how we joyously do and are done.

RED FLOWERS IN THE KITCHEN

no separation

                                                                                        a poem is not about

but I wish to praise the red chrysanthemums
        standing in the cutglass decanter whose top I lost
        that Donald Fuller gave me when he moved
                (from 62nd to 27th St.
                      in New York City)

their red

        really red and ruddier
        now at evening in the artificial light
        against the yellow and white
                      checkered tablecloth
    than in the morning when I bought them.

but description is no praise
        how can I invent their redness in the poem
        to carry calorific color to your eyes

        who are beyond description too.

EGG BREAKFAST

Mornings I eat my eggs

ignorant of my eggs

their shifting auras and devices

hints and prohibitions.

They are only chicken eggs of course

that whisper egg commands

holding in their foreign mouths my forming day.

I like eggs soft boiled

two minutes maybe I don't count

to scoop with spoon hot from shell

like a little white and yellow thrill.

Guys who aren't with eggs I'm not with them.

BALLET

The day dawns in its storm,
a gladness of the sun,
and I dance w/ it.

THE RED-MOUTHED GREEN PARROT

so pretty, green stalks of spinach, pink root attached,

lying on the kitchen table,

sweet taste of late autumn in the mouth

swirl of bright red and orange leaves outside:

       go sweep away big dusty summer;

       spinach sympathizes with the fall.

ON THE RIGHT USE OF SIMPLES

for Tom Meyer

    The meadow was the dream you did not have, you said,
but I was wading in the stream that flows there,
        gathering
                cress and calamus,
                          hot

        in the black waters under my feet
                          the moon.

If your mouth is dry, the berries of the meadow will sweeten it,
    safely enough if you only remember
  that "creatures unfit for human consumption
      are not of the normal order of nature,"

even to think of them is dangerous.

        Of the godly uncanny it is wise to beware.

TO THE BOY CHARIOTEER

        You care
                for the steeds, not victory,
unusual,
       in one so young.

(You are, like me, a real gone time-despiser, forgive the youth-word "young.")

           The rhythm of this arrant purple age
           diminishes the merely actual,
           lineaments of incidence
           or cast of human dice into a bed.

But my intensity for you,
Euphorion,
however privately expressed,
will not diminish,
so faithful is not only memory
but working of the body energy divine.

        Golden was an early word for all of it.

Emerging into sunlight
I dance with capability;
my feeling is a waterfall
that spends without exhaustion of the source.

In Eden, where our dreams of happiness are carefully conserved,
stored as juicy essences the virgin of the world put up,
we eat each other endlessly,
apples sadly rarely shared in what is unjust history.

But we are not asleep in Beulah land.
We live in heat and pain of being here or there,
and if we are slightly nuts it is division wrenches us.

        The Horses, the Horses, black and white!

        See them flying

                  over the chasms of no-love

            their manes are flaming in the night.

They guide your chariot of golden stars,
my cardiogram,
        hold well the reins,
        and pray that so I do on earth as well.

IN THE LIGHT OF THE TINCTURES

Dawn rocks with light as his rocks go off into the mouth of the sea.

A virgin hurls them from cinnabar cliffs.

>Something got into my left eye
>I cannot get it out,
>it is your body,
>and it makes me rub my left eye
>
>When my right eye twins it
>the two of you will sail up into my brain
>my eyes will be soothed
>and my head will not be sore.
>
>The two of you will rock in the hammock on my
>   old-fashioned porch
>holding hands
>loving yourself.

(How mysterious!   What I just wrote as if it were future
              seems to be what has happened already
and I realize that time
              (I had said it before but forgotten)
is not where we really are.)

A bird is flying into a golden cage,
singing of far Mount Abora.
The cage door is always open.
The virgin is the master of the golden cage,
master-mistress comforter of birds
and gives her birds liberty and they come again.

It is night and the poem is ready to end and reform into dawn.

>A man lies on some bed of furious darkness,
>between his legs a kneeling boy.

>Soon the color of the boy's flesh will change,
>from red it turns to blue, to black, then red and white.

He becomes a virgin with a golden cup.
She gives her birds to drink from this cup.

She walks on the cinnabar cliffs.

In the man's clenched hand dawn bursts.

GOLD COAST TANKA

Red Florida sun,
loud indelicate farmer,
why this frantic pitch?
Elsewhere you behave *with,* man,
ripening soft chromatics.

TODAY

A theory of the light,
of color happy,
escape from fuzz,
a litany.

A DRINK

So
old people grow old.
Who knows everyone in the world?
We try, I try, you
   she and it tries.
No progress from the
   Latin tongue.
This is the drink of sensibility, of sense.

HABITS

                                      (who hasn't?
                                    or DOWN & OUT

"Ptarmigans
            haunt
the lofty heights
                       of mountainous countries
in Europe, Asia, & America
descending
                  within the range of vegetation
to feed on berries, buds of trees, insects
                                            &
                                                              etc.

This I found in Webster's dictionary, ed. 1881.

VIII.

PERISHING REPUBLIC

THE WIZARD OF OZ IN THE BLIZZARD OF OZ

For Ken Irby

1. "I am from Kansas
    and the Holy Land of Kansas…"
    —*Ken Irby, at the Glass Sailboat Café, June 19, 1999*

"I've had a sufficiency."
"Oh you've been fishing?"

"No, I said I've had plenty."
"Oh, you caught twenty?"

"You are a Fool."
"You broke your pole?"

The fishing pole is broken, like the sword at the hilt.

Broke, the Central Bank.
Bespoke, hot land of heartland,

too hot to handle
till cooled by the Blizzard of Oz.

Oz is for the strong who are strong enough to be bent,

the bent, the bending, overcome the strongest jock.

Say not no to flow.

2.

       Gasoline prices under federal scrutiny.

       63% of men are dreaming of barbecues
       16% are dreaming of golf
       21% are thinking of car speeds

       A man from Chicago died when a tree fell on his car.

       Revenge of the Nerds.

          The upshot is this:

                      Middle West
                      has evanesced

                      what is left:
                      corrosive sublimate

                      &
       the Wizard of Oz is
                out in the Blizzard of Oz

                      &

       Get OUT is written in the Book of Lies.

out in the Blizzard of Oz

3.

    John Kendrick wrote these words, 1908 maybe:

    Onward Christian Soldiers, rip and tear and smite
    Let the gentle Jesus bless your dynamite.
    Splinter skulls with shrapnel, fertilize the sod
    Folks who do not speak your tongue deserve the curse of God.

  And these are think tanks:

American Enterprise Foundation
Heritage Foundation
CATO Institute
Center for Strategic and International Studies
Competitive Enterprise Foundation
Council for Social and Economic Studies
Center for Security Policy

                Think tanks stink tanks
                                    they advance.

4.
Bettering

I dreamed the money changers owned America, renamed it Equity Plaza.

They plan to surface the earth with asphalt or the most recent product "better" than asphalt.

Each new product has to be better.

Bettering bettering, well smeared with money,

money that now is electrical impulse,

not a substance to touch

better and better

not a substance to feel

nothing to chew on or suck.

5.

        The older you get the more messages from the dead you may receive without perceiving them.

6.   Squeezy Lemon Rejoinder over Disunited
       States

   "the squeezy lemon rejoinder is
    broken at the hilt." — Out to Lunch

Broken at the hilt. Skepticism and historical brain food.
Candied phenomenological retort: bah!
me, moo for family values, ooh!

  Moo, the Mauve Zonule opens:

    I vow by the Cow of Chicago
    to unhinge the evident
    let be seen green
    virulent seething sub urbe to liquidate monuments.

  Let others appoint the beauticians of rust

Yes a tiny purple gender bender flaps on my key ring
as I insert the car key.
No one lives a drug free life, I mean no one.

  Who pilled the tubby custard?

    Hello Central, you gave away Kansas
    once rocker exploding in blood
    heavenly blue and humid, pit beef depot.

  Dotty, Male-in-Female Heroine returned
  where spectres stalk the streets searching emanations out

  weedy gingham fuckups, eyeballs torn.

    Fool was a hero
  before expansion destiny in boobs and balls
     proudly national
  made hick
      mamafesta.

■■■

There are holes in the sky you see certain countries of heaven through the holes

    if you're lucky-unlucky.

       They talk down through my mouth, who

    and how *are* you how *are* you, or how are *who*!

      The gainsayers are here already, they are big in
        the butt and signify.

      We are bringing erasers to work
      we will not need them in heaven
      not need anything at all.
     Remember to forget.
Lights out for the territory, Kansas flaked out in the Blizzard of Oz.

      Over the hills and far away
      Teletubbies come out to play

   Do not count the numbers when you come

7.   EH

>It begins and ends in bamboozle

>fuming in delightful delusion…

kra, the tough realization transcends

without tempering, all things are brahman

>after such sky

>>no transcendence involved in transcending

>>>it is there but not clear
>>>and you cannot be clear

>>>my lord, my mother, my friend

>>who is naming the naming of namelessness?

THE COMPOST

I was speaking, he said, of American poetry,
or was it the other way round,
the way under the hill?

The snowy eye is absolute,
the measure sustaining is never provisional,
majestic it opens on silence.
So the forefathers looked,
and this is the dream of the effulgent republic
without question of affluence.

Their advice to young men:
        WILL   DARE   DO
                      &   SHUT UP
    (.period.)
                      ABOUT IT

has been prized, even by those to whom the name of John Marshall
                            is mud or an elegant rumor,
    for how it pertains to the ART.

That the rebirth of the republic is not eagerly awaited
                          admits of no doubt,
                 but the fact is redoubtable,
                    redounding,
in the speeches of labor leaders and other emmenagogues,
                          of history ignorant.

Such conditions enhance the Men of the Secret
who care for the compost in winter,
waiting to ready the fields.

To attend the currency in votive weather behooves :
viridescent the triangle floats over the altar.
                       Offering made.
                       It has snowed.
                       Poverty drifts in massive installments
through villages, operas, sex never imagined in the dreams of John Marshall,
work undertaken without prospect of gain
                             (unnatural work, which the republic itself
        turned out to be,
            stupid and savage as an intractable poem.

       Ain't pleasant to work at the compost,
       but the niches are empty,
       and the Eye will terribly blaze from the triangle
       when the lion god
                         at last
                                   steps forth by day.

IN THE AMERICAN FOREST

the blest vacant mind
                  inane
  no watercourse of tumbling thoughts
formerly rare in American forests,
           16th to 19th century,
now comes to recognize itself its value,
        burden of Nagarjuna.

Glooskap was busy,
no time to be empty,
working, fighting, shaping,
that the animals be smaller
than in his original error he made them,
adapting all to human universe.

———

The condition is superordinate,
                20th century,
                    a new dogma nears.
Who hails the superhuman I attend.
It is not love one speaks of here,
rather gods known to us by similar name.
See them bend their bows!
Ai, ai, they are sighting their human targets!

  We try to forfend such malefaction
  who identify,
  mistaking secondary personalization
  as if it were actual
                and private.

No privacy left, nor should be,
en plein jour all feeling,
Reclamation
           as of American forest.

Indian is no accidental
          word the Indies
    are connected West and East in mind
subsuming in concurrence
          as of Greece   Sicily
      Europe and America
               AMERINDIA
       the bitter flow.

the forest first philosophers
    (emerging now again as forests disappear)
intone the path of life and death and life   :

the gates, a jar, a jewel in morning mirrored red.

GOOD GOO IN SOOTH

certes,

        I said "certes"

this brandied apricot jam hath too little brandy in it,

no fire to wake the lower skyey wheelings

                        let them wail

    crimson loin birds of glory.

Yet
      a time of seeming plethora in sooth it is

      (in these disunited colonies or states of buzz,
      electronic, undistinguished, electrum lost
      and plethora means apparent choice).

Certes
                whose is choice? (that juice)?
                are you free to scan a sky
                hung with figures of the dead
                a long gone laundry line?

Can you remember mother's eyes,
the cup, with hands of doomful grace?
How steady are you on your feet
when great-great-great grandparents call you to come?
And can you come with spasms of the ghosts
                huddled in cave or under tree?

    Again, the Ark:

                certes

        there is no sailing but into marmalade

                in a time of marmalade.

      Booms gather to fall down

            in rounds of exit

         exeunt omnes the signposts read

and though you might beware the child's hairy watch,

octopoid attention span of her expunging breath,

    certes,

  it is time to overcome your fear of goo,

  come and taste the good goo stew.

READING "MY LIFE" ON A GREYHOUND BUS FROM BOSTON TO NEW YORK

"The world makes one itch, and the scratching makes one warm."
— Lyn Hejinian, one word misread

Better than Virginia Woolf, as good as Emerson,
he thought, letting the sentences sink down.
I am person as description does.
If all the world personifies
and skies are soft as silk
and Mother is a ptarmigan
where *will* we find the milk?
And so
I go
on my quest for the heavenly cow.
  People here
(today, U.S.A.)
don't revere
enough.
("inside," he sighed.)
Revere Beach is so miscalled.
Public reverence is no good, thrush;
pubic reverence is sensible. Hail the pubic arch.
It is a peachy day.
Reverence for peaches, that's my poem.
My life is a big subject, but she tackles it,
and so do some of us, each in our toothsome way,
or ghoulish, foolish, whatever the river.
Once I could run circles around the city block,
but no longer, that's to say the eye that sees
in this poem is of a certain age, as well as certain moving places of.
All places move, swerve, and wheedle.
"There are contemporaries not perceptible":

his whole philosophy was based on that,
but who said it in Sumeria?
Without a hat, the song goes on,
but he sings a wizened song,
rhyming "on" and "ong",
as if the nest were best,
and there's a time to nest and time to test the air,
bird there.
Coleridge my love wrote monologues he called conversations
and conversation is the secret life of stones.
They tumble at the back of the head
to be composed to be composed
as the landscape twitches by
and by its itching forces us.
Willows passing yellow in Connecticut.
The meaning deepened as the morning's grace continues to enchant.

WILL GLEN BURNIE NEVER PASS AWAY?

The bus slowed.
Ozymandias looked around. Ouch!
The horse he rode was a horse with no name
but it might as well have been Camel.
He rubbed his… (erasure) sleepily.
He saw Glen Burnie.
No it won't, "pass away," that is,
who are you to think "taste" will better itself,
especially "human taste"?,
though a better butter does exist,
supposedly in foothills of Coromandel.

Supposing is a Gila Monster Ozymandias supposed,
as he featured meeting the Gunslinger in Katmandu.

Is this Tombstone, Arizona? Ozymandias asked.
The Bus Driver: "No, it's only Asbury Park."

"Well, let me off here,
my little horse must think it queer,
but I see an opening in the sea,
a job I mean, even if it's only sand blowing in the wind.
Here I mean to make my pyramid."

And in Glen Burnie the horse and Ozymandias got off the bus.

                (on a bus going to Baltimore, Md. 1978)

PORTRAIT OF A POETASTER, AND GENTLEMAN OF AMPLE MEANS

He lives in his tower of bread,
eats everything breaded:
      his chops
      his fish
      his broccoli,
      even his bread.
What he writes is well bred,
white and refined,
fortified well with ironic love.
At his bread soirees
he sits on a sofa of bread,
pours bread tea,
leaves unfinished sentences, crumbs.
He brushes his teeth with bread,
sleeps on a bed of bread,
even turns bed boys to bread boys.

Somewhere, in the mountains, real thunder rattles,
young men are hungry.

Slowly, deploring the System
      (Alimentary),
he eats.
      He digests.

QUATRAIN FOR CONTEMPORARY "AMAZING GRACE" STANZA COLLECTION*

When all the malls go up in flame,
    and jails the mighty built,
then we the newly free proclaim
    the Law: Do What Thou Wilt!

*from "The New Amazing Grace," compiled by Ed Sanders
and performed at St. Mark's in Manhattan, fall of 1994, fall of 1995

THE UNDERTAKING

Don't ask where is Wisdom to be sought as ecstatic music sounds and
 the loving republic lies rotting away
in polarities confounded, the rites broken and swallowed by
 public drunkards,
abominable tones sounding everywhere, Capitol to fairy tale
 Radio City Music Halls,
agriculture only ownership,
the ministers administers adverteasing heartsease.

Just don't ask.
I won't tell, am feeding my lamb by the still waters,
but She dances, the Old Girl, yet, where, in the Presence
and She is the (moist) breath of the godly powers and love is the
 keeping of Her laws
and She is empty of own-marks, unstopped unproduced. She sings,
 a lotus blue:

"More precious am I than precious stones a treasure that faileth never
this household is disordered but I am the (sweetly) order of things
and I am Temperance and Prudence,
 as men can have nothing more profit in their life than Me."

IX.

PORTALS

IN ERASMUS DARWIN'S GENEROUS LIGHT

            for Thorpe Feidt

1.

Erasmus Darwin would have agreed with Wilhelm Reich and
   Robert Ingersoll,

        "Better rot in the windowless tomb
              without a door but the worm's red mouth
    than wear
              the jewelled collar
                     of a Mental Slave."

He saw how Joys were trampled in the priests' black rounds
       twisted by quibbles
                of ministers and schools
       knotted secure
                in the jovial social web commodious
       where mystified misery hides
       in starspangled gleams of beautified credit
       and repo men swing
                in Death's tremendous porch

2.

Such a mouthful. How do you put it?
This way the gnostic garden.
Orgonomic functionalist fields forever.
And will he come again, Christ, sexual habit?
Heavy meat knows no vacuous constraints,
what does a ruling class do when it rules?
Flog me, show me, you unlimited political bookstore.
Honeysuckle, grape, and orange tremolos.
But courage, isn't it available somewhere?
It grows not in rows, but in beauteous blotches,
a gorgeous gallery of gallant inventions.
Don't expect it where you look for it.
It's out of sight.

3.

Fickle, fickle, document time.
False documentation is still documentation.
You idiots. I trace the history of the worship of document
to that social loss we've long ago suffered
you slaves who should know how to get OUT, open your eyes.
If the bishop ever lifted his head for a moment,
looked at Nature, Erasmus Darwin said,
instead of document, text, "nothing but pages,"
he'd have realized he was talking through his episcopal hat.
Why man, you have only to go and look at the High Force waterfall
not thirty miles from here
to realize it took tens of thousands of years, at the very least,
to carve its course through rock. And faces in the rock.
This earth we live on is older than old, in spite of the bishop.
& in spite of the attack on "within" the reductionists mount
       within remains within
              there's a monkey puzzle tree.
My "spirit of animation"
              I don't want to get rid of it,
Erasmus Darwin said.
    Within the skull the skill
        within the winter dream the whirligig
      within within
            all & everything :
"Ing" supreme rune and secret song of "Ong."
Forget all derivations,
            they dance in happiness,
the early ones down there,
       and this isn't myth of origin
            or oozing essence origin.
Fuck you, Derrida, Erasmus Darwin said,
origin is beautiful as black
and centers whirl around us as we round them in.

4. *Telluris sacra theoria*

If you consider the sacred theory of the earth,
water below and water above,
the egg cracked and split, the spirit spurting out
flood and ark of sacred origin, waterfall of starry jism
the milk of the stars from her paps
on uplifted ecstatic faces and lovers locked in happy freedom in their
    crucible…

in my garden, Erasmus Darwin said, blooms
bright surprise galore on bright surprise
and from their volant passion splurge cataracts of eyes.

In the tulgey wood the light consoles
and in the generous light of Erasmus Darwin's ripe exuberance
(and he knew the caves below where sun at midnight shone)
the fields, his very strawberry fields, are Eleusinian.

STANZAS OF HYPARXIS

1. In the child's game implacable,
   Imperium on Luna,
   if not a bug-eyed leap
   a giant step at least
   to be eaten with breakfast food by children,
   as matter of fact as that,
   crackle of product in a dish.
   The boy wipes his mouth, empties himself for school.
   Arm-Strong, so.
   Autumn arches in his blood,
   lions quiver in the aura.
   Running in blue light
   the hunter's moon will eat his mind at night.

2..   No time but has its blazon.
		I saw a beacon that seemed intended
		and whose intention was unquestioned.
		The craft is governed by such midnight fires
		as it coasts
		the rocky headlands
		in waters of Attic clarity.
	"On the wind-tormented point,"
	End-of-Earth,
	"and about the shores and islands of the Gulf of Morbihan
	   … gigantic circles and alignments"
	recall an "energy
	born of terrible adventures."

3. Plays with himself
puer ludens
in the secret attic of discovery
revisiting
the pleasure beyond death.
Energy animated and set free the moon sucks up
and from the dormer window
over the harrowed trees
he sees her firmly sit the bucking shadows.

4. The man voyages and is not a child.
The islands are not numberless or nameless.
They stand up in the dawn.
Vigilance to catch perception,
note the flash of fish-scales
in diaphanes of water rush,
this is a craft of holding to,
to make a poem of clashing rock song even
from rocks that mirrors break into the sun.

5. Virginity is to develop
it is the secret power of the male
though may be hidden in a female husk.
Has naught to do with coming or going
but with the set to make a soul.
Not a child's dream
whom black tongues drag to a covered pit
by beat of drum
to be eaten by the Bitch.
Virginity is the mystery,
not yet understood,
of the orgasm from the Thirteenth Cycle
whose hierophant is Ophialtes,
shining in fire
many-mirrored.

6. The long body of the solar system
(seen from the black watch tower),
a polyphase transformer
to step down,
according to each planetary coil,
the energy of the father sun,
create those conditions that inform the wanderers;
in man nine centers glandular
to receive nine modes of sophic fire.

7.   The heavens declare.
         Apophainetai!
 These stanzas do not illustrate ataxia.
    I conjoin mottoes opposite:

     man; child –
     sun; moon –
    hyparxis, dream –

  as emblems requiring mind-work,
nexus buried.
    Wisdom as such hides in the news of the day.

   (Ataxia: this is not
It turns out all to be hyparxis – even dream,
       a ladder of lights.

  The imitative boy is discovering man.
    Sex on earth is rhymed angelic motion.

Outer space and inner space misnomers
     when what is meant (nomen, numen)
  is rhymed in megalith and microspore
  and mirror is parity non-conserved
        so
    go right and left
       go aft, go fore
   go one and two
   and heaven blue.

  In pun conjoined:
    Attic; attic –
    discovery –
    craft; craft –
    mirror; parity –

     From this chimaera, purity?

        Something is hidden.
There are no other words,
               lymphatic power
                       is of the moon
        and must be.
                Her nodes define the zodiac.
                    Terella, ever.   Weather.

But the solar heart defines the blood

                    How far out you go
    it is within.

WHEN LOCALITY FAILS

In the freedom of the greenest rain
only fluctuate
let the fluctuation grow
and surprise is where you fly supreme.

                                 Swooping and looping
you taste the magic mango as a child
and the spring were forwarding your load.
Complexity is not just having a lot of parts
related locally in non-simple ways:
green gene tyranny is divinely free.

                           Only fluctuate,
     auto-erotize, tune in, not forget,
              and emerges a new decisive property

                      quasithermodynamical

                                   playful

                   tiptoploftical

         and your multiverse

                teetotally

                     tintinnabulates

   as former parts, PONG, cohere anew.

CONVENTICLE

The people of the Phoenix do not say "the Phoenix"
and we do not name the Mystery that weaves a parsley garland for the
   temples of the lusters

(Marshes   mothers
the sweet flag fallen and parades move by.

A god is of the nature of the slime;
he invincibly uprises until on surface of the water suddenly is
   Water Lily and the Child.

Eaters of the Lotus

A man cannot be but enters in some folly:
if he is saved the direction and the savor is the god who blind as
   Orphics say and dumb is still the Chariot

we ride in every day
or drown.

TABERNACLES

Over the seagulls and the gull white roofs the music lies like heat
to sound and evidence the blessing of the god
who inhabits where he favors.   Sanctity
returns to place, and time picks up the savor of the merely actual.
Sexual is almost godly on the beach.
The stars are seamen in the hero blue night ancestors
who lean through windows of the high school genitals to certify
   a desperate shibboleth,
Pudenda!

Honor is for thieves to countenance
as the polity of fish and salt evaporates,
and religion universalized: sea salt in old men's eyes who burn
   horizons endlessly in hope to see the coming of the lissome blond

Conquistadors!

The splendid and abasements of the ages come to this:
the body of a man or woman robed in faith and mercy seat of gold
   and ark of testimony.

I have seen the wounds where godhead was expelled:
god needs body and burns in unjust anger until the man is faithful
   and his work be satisfied.

RUMORS

I.   When the last Emancipation Proclamation had been issued, dolor was general in the metropoles: barber shops invaded by headless men demanding endless haircuts, ungodly cantos posted at crossroads. By noon the vendors of flowers had poisoned themselves. Unions dissolve, and high in the mountains the voice of the unicorn!

II.   Unsound voyager in various sleeps, he stumbled drunkenly through a wasted civilization, where lions lay rotting in silkworm granaries. The third eye of a red-faced person had opened in anger, and death rays had swept the chattering tenements and tittering palaces. High whistlings, origination unknown, hourly shattered the needle-like bones of the silence, whose structure slowly reformed in the colorless dusk.

    What gifts had a mother forgotten?

III.   Exploding coffins. Ring of brown feet. Leaves flare to feather an infinite fall. The witches of earth have unsealed the salt mines. No more the fatiguing casinos. Omens hang in the closets.

    I saw a thin lady embracing her future, a giant simplicity.

    Asia! Asia!

    Freedom, new cereals, white canticles unheard, strangers springing from spaceships.

THE BELT

      from Erebus and Terror under ice
north with a swing
              to the East
     under Tierra del Fuego,
                 up along the Andes to
  the Antilles
       under Mexico
             under the Rockies to
Alaska!
    hits to the west,
              Kamchatka and
  down Japan from the Kuriles
                1. out to sea (Philippines)
        branching
                2. down the coast by Ryukyu Isles

  joining up again
        off Indonesia
              cutting West,
through New Guinea
        round Australia, New Zealand and
home again,
       Erebus and Terror.

The burning hell mouth opens to the starless night.

FESTIVAL SONG (THE NEW YEAR)

Look, the man of rain is burning!
Everywhere are dancers turning.

Children memorize their friends
                As they go
                As they go
   Turning intricate and slow.

Look, the man of rain is burning!
The black and winter moon is falling.

Children white and glittering
                Whet their knives
                Whet their knives
   On their rampant private lives.

Look, the man of rain is burning!
The flame is blue as early morning.

Each child takes his lovely peer
                With tender fright
                In tender fright
   They make sharp love and live in shocks of light.

SONG (THE AUTUMN FESTIVAL)

Golden mummers, go away
Red garden blood is cooled to gray
Golden mummers, go away

Goodlooking favorites, goodbye
The moon is sick, the fountains dry
Goodlooking favorites, goodbye

All things go underground with glee
The sun is pale, and under sea,
On earth, in air, in green or flaming tree,
Love massacres his family.
All things go underground with glee.

EQUINOCTIALL (I)

Who attends the darkness in the tree,
reservoir of silence not pulled by sunlight in the leaves,
a boding depth,
also notices the errant wind of March,
how it bodes without ado,
vivifying red disruption all around,
ambush in the Easter egg.
Winter is undone
as old men turn to schoolgirls in unmolding sun
and "Du bist meine Morgen" comes vanilla lisp from bright athletic boy.
It's such a late late show,
couples in the bosks again,
licensed cemetery beds aglow,
old folks at home.

Way down yonder, that's somewhere else.
Here no harvest of finality,
a final party coming out in grand debut
or reeling in.

Just dying fish,
laughter of the giddy monkey on the cross.

EQUINOCTIALL (2)

It was to the bottom of herself the shadow sank,
    where whirling stilled,
    where nothing was recalled.
        It was not inviting even,
        was no connection made
            to anything above that wants to fall
            until the end of falling be assured
            and evening come and novel stars.
In all this no reference to signature
or difference made betwixt
the former fool and latter love
whose shades dressed by ceremony's light
as on the last full day of summer
join in one figure, sarabande,
to hail rebirth of chaos' brother:

his coming forth by night
empowered by latency long foreboding
in harmony of underground
where husks sightless walk as stones at noon.

THE CUTTING OF THE LOTUS

Underneath the underground tree
Shamash and Tammuz in the shade.

I cut the lotus stem. I place the flower in a bowl of clear water.

To name is to count. You will hear a golden bell.

Gone from Iowa the wild turkey, quail,
but still the dentist operates, the boy's sex stiffens,
a Winnebago holds the tooth in his dripping hand.
It is a pearl he gives him.
Under the pillow and it is gone, but re-membering is hot,
the manitou's hot breath on the pillow stone at Luz.
He gives to all who enter once to take the seed of heaven
to enter twice into a place of wind and water,
it is named the country of ripening stones.

To name is to portend. As we are given names.

The hen held upside down, with my right hand I push her head down
to lay it on the block. The hatchet is keen.
Sun warm on my bare shoulders,
chicken's head in straw and dirt and chicken dirt.

To name gives you know what. I will not tell you how to eat
    the pomegranate.

The roots are black and muddy at the bottom of the lily pond
where water and mud are not separated.
No tenses. The words tumbled from all the mouths of the god at once.
He rubs himself with his utterance. He shines.

Out of the dunghill a cock scratches the pearl. To give to the
   philosopher.

The dentist chuckles, gnaws his bone, listens to the pounding of the
   proud piano.
The boy and girl explore the empty rooms above the stable where now
   the chariots are kept.
Up the back stairs!
                   Rubedo!
                                 Slain by the pleasure beast!

That there some death, tongues, rainbow bodies rainbowing.
Shot. Blood in my mouth. The proper nouns. Hear.

Shamash and Tammuz together in the shade. Their fingers touch.
The stars are hot in the branches of their tree.

OLANA
OR, THE SHARK OF CRAVING

    I.   ZAMINDAR

Of all agenda not mechanic
mine is critical as any.
Starting out from Cordoba
as tingling signals
                        mint snakes
      as I do,
         Ida,
            here.
Purple water of the rotten grapes.
Plotted chance meetings define the novel,
                        lovers,
              novel lovers.
De novo.
          Great Ida will reappear,
man-mountain,
        when you bang a rite.
In the conduit walk east.
      Beacons of prana
move up and down
           in my feeling
     as I sit in siddhasan.
      In Cordoba the Arabs
tickle European testicles.
  Like limitations, my life,
painting one flower all life long
concealing real infractions in
               benign aggression
taking advantage of steam.

      Selah.
           Like limitation,
                seemed unlimited
          the seed
    inward so,
    what *they* called dream
    or dream
    or dream retreat.
                My forest.
      After dhanur,
        utthita kumarasan.
I swallowed the personal key.
It has dissolved.
Smart dope and I distinguish,
        TAKING ADVANTAGE OF STEAM
    the funeral amulet:
    say Zu Zu to the grocery boy!
A cacophone: cordoba shit.
Crumpled ferns for feet
        the juice that shrinks
even at even tide.
Ataraxia my sister…
I gather the taxes due reality.

Artaxerxes the brother lost
      because never known
      spiralled down a time
      I never shunned,
      not spanned,
the twin I missed
semblable abrazero!

The wish to be cowboy,
    devotee,
           and zamindar.

II.   HOT BREEZE AND BLUE MOON

the shivering milk
            plush faces
made of beds
the Five-M Company
            entered the banquet

Ida pirouettes, a jumpy kid

      compulsive rectangles arise

I lick the semiologic ice cream cone
                        divine.

Transparent as an upchucked butterfly
      the lamination held,
          gone buffalo,
in heaven as a toothbrush.
      Who is steering anyone?
She drank Blue Moon,
      gnawed a pomegranate,
Persephone,
      then danced the Cassava
            to Mambo Mania,
    loins like a brooding cloud.

What houngan wears "Cherchez la Femme"
as wheat scoundrels chew their nails
and masturbate racemes of light.

Bluehaired dragonettes
           unveiled the registers.
    some chophouse!
        where a stingy demiurge
              dropped the sugar cubes.

Cones impact. Ice cream skull crack.

Old anise drugstore cycled into whiteness of
        Hollywood too long gone in memories of tigers,
           harp concertos,
     supple long-haired Holland boys

   TAKING ADVANTAGE OF STEAM
hitting Orion highs
             you rock the course
     until it juices
         like a splitting box.
These fangs could do you anything.

I slept in the tree of Samkhya
     after filming the stars
  La Féerie Orientale.

Stamped to see the butterfly,
              who did?
In the stone orchards of memory
     his young voice rang out,
"Breathe, don't forget to breathe."

    Concentered,
             of pineapple throat,
            what melodies?
Glowing, having fixed up
   ecstacy,
    one boy came quickly in the sink,
    as mint snakes wriggled there.
"Severo, my love," another moaned,
            "and Vladimir …"

Let's ooze. Lotus lay. Ida's back.

    immense dropping glitter stalk

        Bhang trees, bhang fruit,
coot walk, cut.   No cat.
      or outis, soham.

Coin your catchwords, cunt.

Eat, eat my kind real god
     gold weathercock, you boy!

      This apple is to fly.
Behold the great empty beauty of intractable being!

To be is not to what you think I say
      was saying
    just now
           NOW

III.

Taking advantage of steam
this cantata is for potentates!
A coda of mistletoe come.
Oblate spheroids, boys!
      Ida, goddess, mint julep is my name.
         in Olana ashram as here,

To be is not not-not what you think
      I wasn't saying, now not

        just

            now!

              Δ

THE END OF NATURE IN THIS WORLD

The third mother kindles in the darkness of concordance
and fierce in qualifying comes the wrath
(sic rerum summa novatur semper)
boiling from the spring,
black, spew of Mimir's head,
murderous astringency,
bruising eyes in fire cracks and fracture of humanity.
    Flick.   Block.
 Relief from wheels, beg, o beg
       good dancing at the gates
   to make the gates fall down
     now the 13th angle of the crystal capable,
    so nails once fast now fall away,
      all sticking bolts or bars,
   and never will be shut again.

Let winds flow in and out,
      Boreas, Favonius,
  fountain spirits murmuring,
      Eurus, Apeliota, Notus
kissing, relishing, begin.   Rollick,
  be gaily quizzical, neutralities,
  the world is yours to eat it up:
  never belonged to *anyone at all.*

CINQUAIN: BETHEL

mountain
of the Lord's house
slowly reaches up to
(& never to be lightning wrecked)
the stars

THE MANY-WORLDS INTERPRETATION

(from the Egyptian

God stiffened;
hand rubbed up and down his mighty Member:
world upon world cascades from his cock.

THE GOLD IN THE MUD

      legendary darkness in the dayshine,
      how it works to be,
      sleeping on the floor,
      how bodies love.
              shrewdness of it,
              of being in time,
        what it takes to know
        what gnosis is,
        that our knowledge
            exceeds our having minds,
            newspapers of fate,
not madness but logic of the rites of whatever seasons come to be.

    (A scribble,
        as might a shepherd say,
      whose sheep are human sheep.

IALDABAOTH

LORD OF THE STARS,   of this world,
from whom we derive inequity,
who make the bow and lyre one,
        sickness to pleasure health,
        weariness to pleasure rest,
        hunger pleasure pleromatic gusto:

a girl in a blue dress,
        weaving soothly in the cool night air,
            twines what little can be said against you.

THE OGDOAD

        the sun ship mounts
only when the heavenly serpent spits his seed to the earth,
        the vine springs forth
        as Eden and Elohim dream.
the fixed stars have to shoot up abilities day by day
        to go on gliding on golden rails of appetence.
This is called the Worsening of Time.
        the redeemed redeemer stands in the bow
        passes by,
            knowing the passwords,
            having wrestled in the mud,
            and afterwards,
                    passing by.
      "one power
          divided above and below
          multiplying itself
          looking for itself
          finding itself,
          dad and mom in one."

    Vulgarities do not intrude
                guitars play in heaven
                          and saxophones

so the living word only lies in play of love
            and as we pass the eight
    the numbers take themselves into their spaces,
            all menaces evert themselves.

ENTHYMEME

1.

    and as and the bodiless
    turning in the green not not beripe
    not by autumn not turned on now no
    longer turning earth

    awakes itself to wingless credences
    of buried orchards
    so as and as so circle sings to sleep
    and as not bronze stretches to
    feel a perfect to beyond a bird
    to string a fall of amber burliness
    on wires magnifying and
    human besunk
    (sloth stalks now rapid circuits of decease)
    to as lemniscate once gracious twelve
    blacken in the eve of black
    risen awful head of staring will,
    Her Majesty,

2.

      a spectre wide of will
      and pride of pestilence
      (as if the monogene were sick)
      turning in the white of
      veering absences like violent fish
      as it beckons, simile, a chronic door.

      the spectre strides, so let it,
      sing,
      in kitchen,
      starry spill,
      retracted seed dissolved.

      as to and as to woe in way.

3.

    so and as and reveals a syntax
    principal,
    pauper of a hungry hint.

4.

      hot in visionary clasping
      (again the beckoning fair to fair)
      in mist resolved,
      miel de lune,
      and barbaresque

      she takes your tongue
      into her mouth.

      consonantia
      mollified, dark rest,

      for a time unspecified
      till vibration starts to as and as to end…

BEHIND THE VALE AND IN THE PLEASAUNCE
OF THE PYTHAGOREAN COMMA

      as it were
           twelve intervals of fifths
                covering a little more than seven octaves

I.

    the bride stripped bare in happiness

    exulting in a sounding of the sun,

    house warm and lazy afternoon.

    Of summer redounding in the heights,

    unhappiness suspended in Annapolis, exempli gratia,

    all cities depend from one goddess who delights in seeming various,

    wears exultant livery, she does,

              lingerie or broderie,

  exotically to pique the prick of a rather stupid errant spouse.

II.

This interval, discrepancy,

       does not lend itself to logic

            (because

                     it must be declared, the mystery)

   Logick equals Magick

       (I leave it to you to find what is really meant)

  and in the phone of being where

      I swing and so will you,

only imagined, but not alone,

  independent but resplendent in a bank of flowers,

gleaming in a sudden gaudy bronze,

     athletic, esthetic

      as absurdity,

the final Mathematick, heaven.

III.

        Of heaven, not as lemma,

                not as leaven, but as substance

                    we enfold,

                                we embrace for rational.

                what makes us lovable in deed

                            ———

        There is no equal temperament.

IV.

      A voyage to another,

            as if forever olive trees were arctic,

                a dog relaxing in a chair,

                      a highball.

    Pythagorean because the shells are blue,

                      and blown,

     a blazoned beach of exact

                    lithe

                          particulars.

V.

                There are mothers

                              who work in secret,

                              seriously,

                              but with a smile.

        Serenity is this golden afternoon,

                cats not reflections of a god,
                                          asleep.

      All things come as commas in a cosmic intervale,

          and Beauty proves itself by being so.

WITHOUT DESIGN DESIGN GOES ON

In the dream retort
the wrong,
the death was pure,
mors,
the gnawing of the mouse
"I am" flashed backwards on the screen and disappeared,
pelican shuddered
grey mist covered "the terms" I have to call them
since ain't no word for (dialect of who?)

A new step, requiring no more menstruum of baser sort
(though helpful in other vulgar operations utilizing dogbane say,
low-German or High-Dutch conniving my friend Jonas called them
    once I think,
I phoned to find the words? and for
the making of the poem
he said he didn't know),
male seed possibly still to be used however.
I couldn't make out the form that gestured as the door swung to,
a man with the head of a weasel possibly,
and I shot back into the steaming morning air
fulvescent from the fubbery which wasn't any more than what we cast
    about us every day,
after all
dreck of dailiness,
without our knowing it.

So that's for ritual compressed into a cup.

At any rate, progression, another name,
the day shone today a helmet at the bottom of a well.
I plunge my hand into the water,
cooling,
pick it up and put it on.
My love and I will ride out glittering,
this holiday, this new old spring.

FINDING THE FLAP

As not yet a flip. But flaw
like rift in crystal grows to envelop.
Aslant the brook the willow bends
and cracks, ice riving it.
What was green now brown.
Music buckles. Above your head
the spider web
trembles, ready to catch.
At first not sinister, the left hand
knows what goes wrong aright
and coinheres. Complicity.
Soft as the day, a velvet springe
so all's out's in free.
Speedwell and harlequin spin to snowfall.

X.

THE SOLUBLE FOREST

THE SOLUBLE FOREST

I.

    a "technical study"
    tracking the Numbers
    given the River Map
    and the Riverine Words

        a "technical study":
            Complex Psychology
            Analytic   "
            Archetypal "

                                  :

        the game of Carl Gustav Jung

that naming
        is gaming

II.

who gauges the shadow games?

>I reek I reek
>of *mimologique*

>*

>inaccessible Perfume

Aromatherapy
>you *logophiliques*

>lying in shadowy leaves
>of the floating tree!
>His hair. And her.
>>Ophelia-tree, ophidian crossed!
>>The shadow was lost
>>>till we found it in play.

III.

       in the blazing stadium
           of mirroring thirds

       the word of the law
           is liberty, a book:

          liber - - - legis

a writ is a route.

IV.

    A WRIT is a route, a way and the map of a way. It figures and we make of it our figure, you make of it your figure, I make it of mine. It is mind, and no mind, inner and dinner and outer and doubter.

    Doubtless these figures are crystal.

    From the center of nothing something spreads out, that then there now. From zero jumps two, two being how something is apprehended. Only a stone's throw from writing to root. The rite of winter is the root of spring.

    The house stands on its cellar and grows up. Also grows down from its garret invisibly, as the crown of a tree flourishes the idea of its root.

    Shine, heaven, darken and shine, that the process may stir as things emerge from the void of no-thing. It is plenty. All around us the letters are cast, to be spelt, to be sown like spelt, grain of the garment unseen as green as it makes it.

    Do you, do I?

V.

       Spelt from the mummy's tomb:
                      a cereal poem:

           it die and be
           it comes as it goes

                Eleusinian

VI.

        the Poem
            comes in its own cocklight,
time solary flowering bird sings up the rising god

        He-Who-Comes

              di-wo-nu-so-yo   Zagreus

    Him-at-Home-in-the-Depths-of-the-Sea

        —————————————

      "Neglect not the Dawn-Meditation"

          AUMGN

VII.

     in light of inscribing

To say that life ends in
the violet light
of the straw-bottom chair
is to begin at the end:
where to start out from:
starting out from light,
first breath, first light,
out of the mothering hole
burrow of blood, membranes
flowering rich red,
pulsating, pulsating,
is to ask why start?

start because we *were* started
spinning-tops of desire
not disorder ending in vulgar order,
death,
not either,
rather,
neither nor.

This chair
   charily goes
in the light of this chair
   by flesh inscribed it is,
this hand,
    this chair the pen I hold

in the violet light of
the straw-bottomed chair
that has swallowed the shadows of green and the shadows of red

VIII.

        psyche inscribed in biohologram:

        locating in time is always first step
        and first error is separating
        "environment" from its "going-on-in"

             .

        "the very act of
              and the intention behind
                      observing

              disturbs the observed" *

supraliminal language-field is body-field
      is feeling
            and feeding:

electromagnetic you   Nu-it
                Anagnorisis.

      Schrödinger's cat is out of its box,
      lying in wait for the mouse in the basement:
      what's unbeknownst to us is somewhere beknownst:
      Swedenborg stoops to stroke Schrödinger's cat.

             .

---

   *Lawrence Beyman, "Quantum Physics & Paranormal Events," in *Future Science,* ed. John White.

so I am always finding in feeling
locating in shifting
the terms that compose me
the rhetorical cinnabar lode
whose clavicle's wavicle's key.

IX.

      in exopsychology
      the messenger substance
      figures as figure,
      young bitch and old maid,
      the boy in the sun,
      old man harboring babe,
      etc. etc.
      all decans and images thereof.

      Light speaks the tongue of the shadow.
      Others' dreaming invades our sleep.

      On the genetic clavier
      the genie decodes
      "always remaining subject"

                  and the subject's discourse
                            is the other's unconscious.

X.

      on the wheel
             the buckets communicate,

the gold is poured from one to another, from her to us to me

   to him to them and under the greenwood tree

     the proud shifters prance.

         Dusk, and
             the gate of the tongue is opened,
                the tinctures cross,

   and tomorrow rustles in yesterday's corpse.

      Light the death lamps, see the shadows condense!

Bahlasti! the dust settles
                and the figures uprise.

XI.

    So the river rites are done
                and eleven signifies

                sinless and of us
                   of what traces us
                       and races throughout

  not two, not one, not none

                                    of us,

                and Her again.

XII.

OF SIGNIFYING STONES

There are four philosophic stones Elias Ashmole writes of, in his Prolegomena to his anthology *Theatrum Chemicum Brittanicum*, the Stone Minerall, the Vegitable, the Magicall, and the Angelicall:

1.　the Minerall "the which is wrought up to the degree onely that hath the power of Transmuting any Imperfect Earthy Matter into its utmost degree of Perfection."

2.　…"by the Vegitable may be perfectly known the Nature of Man, Beasts, Foules, Fishes, together with all kinds of Trees, Plants, Flowers, etc. and how to produce and make them Grow, Flourish, and beare Fruit; how to encrease them in Colour and Smell, and when and where we please, and all this not onely at an instant, Experimenti gratis, but Daily, Monethly, Yearly, at any Time, at any Season; yea, in the depth of winter."

Of the Vegitable Stone "the Masculine part of it . . . is wrought up to a Solar Quality, and through its exceeding Heate will burne up and destroy any Creature, Plant etc. That which is Lunar and Feminine (if immediately applyed) will mitigate it with its Cold; and in the manner the Lunar Quality benums and congeals any Animall, etc., unlesse it be presently helped and resolved by that of the Sun; For though they both are made out of one Natural Substance: yet in working they have contrary Qualities: neverthelesse there is such a natural Assistance between them, that what the one canot doe, the other both can, and will perform.

Nor are their inward Vertues more than their outward Beauties; for the Solar part is of so resplendent, transparent Lustre, that the Eye of Man is scarce able to indure it; and it the Lunar part be expos'd abroad on a dark Night, Birds will repaire to (and circulate about) it, as a Fly round a Candle, and submit themselves to the Captivity of the Hand: And this invites mee to believe, that the Stone which the ancient Hermet (being then 140 Years old) tooke out of the Wall in his Cell, and shewed Cornelius Gallus, Ann. 1602. was of the Nature of this Vegitable Stone: For (upon the opening his Golden Box wherein it was inclosed) it dilated its Beames all over the Roome, and that with so great Splendor, that it overcame the Light that was kindled therein; Besides the Hermet refused to project it upon Metall (as being unworthy of it) but made his Experiment upon Veronica and Rue.

3. By the Magicall or Prospective Stone it is possible to discover any Person in what part of the World soever, although never so secretly concealed or hid; in Chambers, Closets, or Caverns of the Earth: For there it makes a strict Inquisition. In a Word, it fairely presents to your view even the whole World, wherein to behold, heare, or see your Desire. Nay more, It enables Man to understand the Language of the Creatures, as the Chirping of Birds, Lowing of Beasts, etc. To convey a Spirit into an Image, which by Observing the Influence of Heavenly Bodies, shall become a true Oracle: And yet this as E.A. assures you, it is not any wayes Necromenticall, or Devilish; but easy, wonderous easy, Natural and Honest.

4. "Lastly, as touching the Angellical Stone, it is so subtill, saith the aforesaid Author, that it can neither be seene, felt, or weighed but Tasted only. The voyce of Man (which bears some proportion to these subtill properties,) comes short in comparison; Nay the Air it selfe is not so penetrable, and yes (Oh mysterious Wonder!) A Stone, that will lodge in the Fire to Eternity without being prejudiced. It hath a Divine Power, Celestiall, and Invisible, above the rest; and endowes the possessor with Divine Gifts. It affords the Apparition of Angells, and gives a power of conversing with them, by Dreames and Revelations, nor dare any Evil Spirit approach the Place where it lodgeth. Because it is a Quintessence wherein there is no corruptible Thing: and where the Elements are not corrupt, no Devill can stay or abide.

S. Dunston calls it the Food of Angels, and by others it is termed The Heavenly Viaticum; The Tree of Life, and is undoubtedly (next under GOD) the true Alchochodon, or Giver of Years; for by it Mans Body is preserved from Corruption, being thereby inabled to live for a long time without Foode: nay 'tis made a question whether any Man can Dye that uses it."

XIII.

                Signifying is butterfly catastrophe

between terminals of certainty, tall terminals
or virtues of the text, procedure a division,
under lilt of waves,
to register is to note the uniform:
this "uniform that music wears when most… ",
such catch in throat or of the eye,
a hit at dawn.
                    Old and new dependencies, good harbor,
deserted beach of seaweed brown
I walk, distinguishing processes and systems…
        mouth is dry to speak a love,
        partition of the waves without exhaustion,
        blue accordian.

    The sky black with derivatives I only mumble,
     the feelings beam, include a solitude
     whose love pores over tables endlessly:
     of action, tablature, guitar, and love
                a music pricked on vanishing.
On Eastern Point and in my head a tree of monarchs
             pullulates
      late butterfly catastrophe .

XIV.

    THE VEIL, and Making the Soul

                                    in American Numbers

        Sister perturbation:

            American desiring-tubes
     sucking in phones and *klactoveedsedsteenotonique*
         for archetypal daedalion.

                  so its Poets (Hers)
                      deal tedium
               unless
                         the Angel of Bethesda
              nods

                 ———

          and not misheard
          and springs to life
          the time of Cotton Mather
          and Hart Crane

                 stirring the pool - - *vibhakti*

  the clutch at
        real hair

		(In England there was no sacred veil
						to go behind)
	here, the inelegant poem,
		hardly time to speak

					of Psyche's chores
			or even drag.

XV.

GOD IN HIS IGNORANCE IS THE FATHER OF LIES

justify the domination by untruth, it does, the ugly myth:
                by untruth the juice that stupefies
                by untruth the cruel barbers' fantasies
                by untruth the cellophanes enshrouding love
                by untruth the dummies
                by untruth the blinded horse
                by untruth your hands chopping my blocks of
                      heart for so much bloody stew meat
              by untruth the whispering handkerchiefs of torturers
  he kisses her under the untrue sign of festival
  he stabs her stabs him stabs their self in riddling stabs
  as what's corruption but that which mystifies
  as it shines undead
  not the mystery or bliss or satisfaction new in gasping overlaps.
To shun,
that is the mission of untruth,
to turn away,
to not attend,
handling the unhanded, down,
the hindrances,
the human sink, the cold and fading colors in, the greasy situation
  bottomless.

XVI.

                towery between….

            and flowers falling….

    every time I come this way….

                the endless….

the work to dissolve

the news of the day in the news of the night

XVII.

HERMES BIRD

    Something is roosting in the hemlock boughs, visible glittering behind the snow, sun rippling in frozen puddles. It is feathered, it roosts, I see the flash of its eyes, it is alert, a many-colored bird.
    It is my zest, making ready there in the green and white tree, ready to move the season a half-turn, turning what was, now nothing, to something else, the pride of surprise unravished by sunset.
    Urgency flutters, the capable bird, lithe agency of glory. The flush of the bird dominates the tree, making it background. The bird can take off, at any time. It brings news from nowhere to nowhere. It is unseizable. Wait till it sings!

XVIII.

                is the number 18

       the tablets are empty

       everybody's crossed over

       and no one has ever gone over

       because always is never because

              utterly utterly gone

       and under the moon

       the swimming forest dissolves

XI.

IN NORTHERN EARTH

IN NORTHERN EARTH

The graveyard overgrown and memory effaced,
cats of many colors run among the sumach
that roots in human stomachs long gone back
to long enduring earth, and what is length
of days or seasons in astronomy of death?
Endurance is calamity if earth speaks true
and the measurement of time is not posterity.
How the line must lengthen while the sun endures
and the poem report advanced celebrity!
Dissolve, coagulate, the chemists say:
but the first darkness blinds the human eyes
that climb the ladder of the visionary spinal chord to issue in
                                          the thousand-petalled sun.

APPENDIX:

THE BURDEN OF SET

STATEMENT: HOW *SET* WAS CONCEIVED

In 1959, when I decided to produce a small magazine, I sent out a note (prodrome) about the magazine's content and format to a number of poets and poet-friends. I said that SET would be photo-offset, appear irregularly. As to intent and content I wrote: "SET will be about the poetic exploration of the swarming possibilities occult and/or unused in American life, urban and local, here & especially *now,* at this moment of the Aeon, i.e. the Vulgar Advent."

"The gates of memory and intuition, history and magic, open from a 'windowless' monad into Time," I wrote Kenward Elmslie, amplifying a sentence in my prodromic statement, "Thus its (i.e. SET's) character will be dual *historical & magical,* the emphasized characters of Time." (The last phrase delighted Robert Duncan.)

"In this time-moment poetry and science meet. Hence the manifesto states that SET is interested in material 'relevant to the poetic-scientific study of American experience and nature…'" but "As I wrote Frank O'Hara, 'I don't want SET to be polemick abt Amerika…will be more James Dean & Andrew Jackson Davis than Marcel Marceau or the Sar Peladan…" I also wrote Frank, "Certainly I want neither the 'monumental' nor the 'study' …the 'study': the nature-morte ou vivante of the Misses Moore, Bishop, Wilbur, etc."

[the datedness of this now entertains me (1997)].

Around 1959 I wrote the poet Steve Jonas that the name of the proposed magazine comes on like or in the places of its play, as:
1. jazz (wch most readers will read as primary)
2. stance
3. direction
4. "theory of Sets" in *mathesis*
5. (tennis, for those who like it)

6.   the God — by the Chenoboskion gnostics
identified w/ the Biblical Seth — and and and
Shem   Melchizedek   Christ   /   Antichrist   Saturn
Typhon   Mercury   Dionysius (sacred ass)   Capricorn

"Enough ! or Too much " (Blake)

— Gloucester, Massachusetts, 1997,
at the Equinox of Fall

Postlude to STATEMENT:

These hortatory "Burdens" of short-lived *Set* (1961–1964) demonstrate what then seemed to a young poet-thinker needful to say about the contemporary situation, what required attention in the "America" of that time.

Today (2009 CE), adit to another Aeon, needful to note new conditions of "writing", reception, and expression opened by electro-magnetic means (computer, World Wide Web, etc.), thence novel generations and coruscations of consciousness. How "publication" must be differently contextualized. The entire social and economic nexus of history and magic requires new phenomenologies, new configurations.

THE BURDEN OF SET #1 (EDITORIAL

Now as the Influx begins to be felt, time to build the arks, to nominate
>proclaim the Qualities

>>In time of the "Breaking of Strength"
>>the burden (droning undersong)
>>is to make the connections
>>inter sed extra

>The Work of the Renovating Intelligence

This magazine is about the poetic exploration of the swarming possibilities (some occult, unused) in American life, urban & local (the rural is no longer available to poetry; to life?), here & especially *now*. Its character is conceived as dual*, *historical* & *magical,* the emphasized characters of Time.

1. *the emphasized characters of Time*

The gates of memory & intuition, history & magic, open from a "windowless" event into Time, the fateful Cross (crux) behind the shifting hexagrams.

To discover our spacetime address we must fix our position in time as well as in space. And this "address" (our mode of being) is personal but also collective: "We are continents if we are." The way Americans, now, receive time differentiates us from others, say Peking man, the ancient Greeks, the Indians. Homogenous time doesn't exist in human experience, our living time is mythically organized, "favored"

---

* See Appendix I to this essay, "The current Prejudice Against Duality," & Appendix II, "Time is (the) Number 2."

by the singling out of "points" distinguished for their values. Since "myth creates time" (G. van der Leeuw), the sense of history as well as of subjective past & future is magically determined, just as the magic appropriate to an age is historically determined.

You have then two ways to take a fix on Time, one by investigation of history, "from the inside out," another by investigation of the dark interiors, "from the outside in," like objectifying an image (magic), the Path of the Names.

This orientation (eastfacing, sunrising) in Time man can only make individually, in his inwardness, but it is not less factual or more imaginative for that: As Wallace Stevens says, "To be at the end of fact is not to be at the beginning of imagination, but it is to be at the end of both."

Thus "poetry increases the feeling for reality" (again Stevens) & the historic fact (our scene) lies equally beneath all the moving poetry & all the moving science we make. Poetry & science invisibly concur between the poles, & the Properties of the World are summarized for any point-moment by the Riemann-Christoffel tensor or by a poem

&

"…in the beauty of poems are the tuft and final applause of science." (Whitman)

2.   *our scene and how it disposes the poem*

Now in these, as Olson says, "dragging years of the fish bones," what is to be hailed?

        The breakthru to the world of forms
                by insight
                by outsight
                by upsight
                by downsight
:   the form of the poem must be our habit

A. for use   now   THE INSTRUMENTS

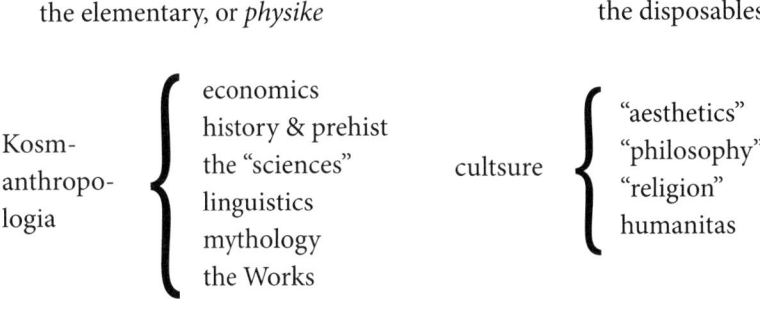

B.   the Knife of Set

The weight (threat & promise) of "artistic" *permanence* or *greatness* is now lifted from the soul of the seer (*persistence* remains an interesting question). Since kulchur is dead (bred cultsureness: that goes on) we are all enveloped by its stink (some poems measure the sensitivity of the nose) but energy at least & at last is free to recognize itself (the work of the 13th Aeon or Sphere or Month).

Poetry falls on an age of undoing like *nothing known before,* & rite measure & metric flow from the crystal of the Moment. Memento & talisman are dimensional of the Influx. The metric of the contemporary must be a gain of form arising from the shift of obedience. Although this shift is in part a displacement from traditional external forms of order to the shape of the person, no doctrine of "personism" or "composition by hazard" need be invoked to the creation of the poem.

"The basis of all metrical determination must be sought outside the manifold, in the binding forces which act on it," the great 19th-century mathematician Riemann wrote, & if applied to poetry, as everything must be sooner or later, this delivers the poet to the full complexity of how he uses what comes in to him. Alchemists & cooks have the same problems, how to manage the heat:

> A parfet *Master* ye maie him call trowe
> Which knoweth his Heates high and low.

Then "image is deficiency," as the Gnostics say, & any typology of poetic "Image" gets hung up on the line of similarity, comparison. (Insofar as "image is referential it means a leak in the vessel, which should be Hermetically sealed for the cooking, *en daube*.)

> The poem had better move OUT

C.   the Path of the Names

The breath of Set may bring "criminal violence," but it also renews, desiccates to freshen.

1484, in Rome, Joannes Mercurius de Corigio, wearing a crown of thorns inscribed "this is my son Pimander I have chosen," preaches, pushes leaflets, proclaims "the new newness of newnesses greater than all miracles." It came to pass.

Now almost 500 years later (Orwell's *1984* itself can give us little, too spiteful too bright lacking the *foolish* wisdoms — but was its date whispered him by the Lord of the Gates of Matter & Child of the Forces of Time?). Again the Revolution of the Quarters, & now the Advent of the Sign of Man.

Mathesis today demands research in the world of letters, combinatorial analysis of the alphabet of the gods. Two books by A.E. *The Candle of Vision* & *Song and its Fountains* contain, among much romantic detritus of the European past, records of "spontaneous" experiences among the Flashing Tablets where language originates.

In the 13th century Abraham Abulafia more systematically studied the Path of Combination, foreshadowed a time like ours when prophecy would be self-confrontation & the magic of inwardness be hidden in the autonomy of the visible, the uses of secrecy obscured, hard to come by.

"In this the things without figures are figured."

Appendix I.	The Current Prejudice against Duality

Such a push toward One & away from Two, among contemporaries, it needs to be said more sharply, 2 yes. There is a formula called the Zero=s 2 equation, not mathematic, & would be mistaken to treat it as such. Process involves the consideration that since it is always possible to reduce any expression to Nothing by taking 2 equal & opposite terms, $n + (-n) = 0$, one should be able to get any expression desired from Nothing by being careful that the terms are exactly opposite & equal, $0 = n + (-n)$. (It is obvious that what is termed in magical work the Equilibrium is a development of this principle.) The 0=2 Formula evades Monism, Dualism, Nihilism, Pluralism, etc. & therefore when it is said, "there are 2 ways," the simplicity of 2 is meant, not not-one, not-three, etc. (two friends to whom I showed early drafts of this essay bridled at any use of the word "dual," one of them saying it was because he "took the Zen standpoint.").

Appendix II.   Time is (the) Number 2

A. That Time is the Number 2

>   twi   di   dvi
>   two   duo   *duwi
>   ti (Arm.)   dayate ("he divides")
>   (opp. in *a*dvaita vedanta

$$\left.\begin{array}{l}\text{time}\\\text{tide}\end{array}\right\} \text{*di}$$

B. That Time is the Number 2

>   di
>   schiz   -   divide, split
>   skhizien
>   schizen (Middle High Ger.)
>   scheissen, scite, shite = No. 2

ergo, Time is "*filthy* lucre"

THE BURDEN OF SET #2 (EDITORIAL

ephphetha
        it is morning

                & you are waking up from a
                dream of fishbones & broken vessels
       to the new attentions
                a new praxis SET
          toward the unfolding of the Moment

by the operation of a scientific illuminism along 2 axes,

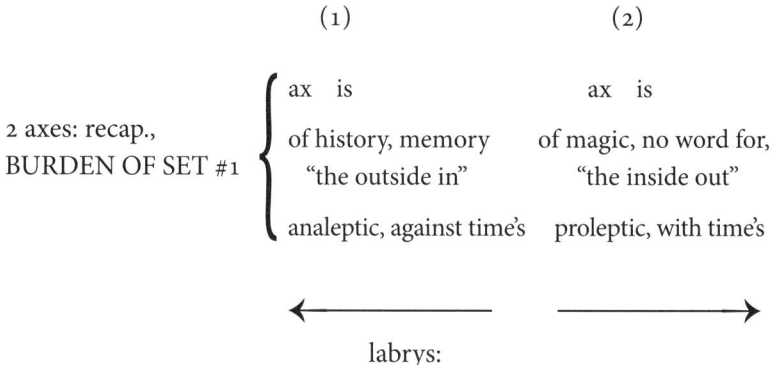

the double ax, & in labyrinths, beginnings, opening of the figures of Time that compose the structure of our necessity, how by poetry we investigate the needs.

1.   *the new attentions*

                                              with (3) GLANCES AT VALUE

o.k. Let it come down, in on us, all of it, so much as we can, & then to get it out again. That was an Epitome of Yoga, inside front cover of SET #1,   "SET still, stop thinking, shut up, get Out," & yoga is concentration of experience (exclusion too, yes, but not of experience itself, rather of experien*ces* not really experienced enough, restraint of the modifications of mind in order to feel their source) whose enemy is abstraction, distraction, retraction, any thing or way that hinders the going traction.

It's traction we are after too, the freedom & recognition of. The enemies, listed in THE BURDEN OF SET #1 as "disposables," all function as guardians of Value, not value as tropism, that we all have, but abstract judgement, ideals.

                                        so

2 discriminations to be discriminated: Value, abstract affective discrimination (1), is the enemy of poetry, & of discrimination (2), of & to, what is out there (pointing), the object, *that*.

Wardens of values, upholders of "crapulous creeds," fear the light of the liberated cortex & the coming ascendency of air.

———————————————————

(3) GLANCES AT VALUE

1.

In an iron age, bitch,
she strides from iron pinnacle to pinnacle, the pinnacles,
clothed in iron robes, unsmiling,
hair is iron gray, bowels tight.
Nightjars play about her splendid shoulders,
her left hand spills the iron jar of equity
her right hand brandishes the iron flail of separation.
Where she is a darkness is and adjectives,
the line is rigid, her patrols are ugly throats.
She is backward to the dawn of universal breath.

2.   Loot, Archetypal Value

It began in ignorance, away from vid-ya,
birth of value in the straw and dung of the 1st (un)stable economies.
Though value never vector, is standard only, there remains the process.
But standard of gold was made gold standard
and when a sign of value (say $)
itself is made a value ($!)
value process desiccates, stands still
turns mechanically in standard
because the normal straight relation
of x the sign (like $)
to that of which it is the sign
grows ghostly, self-reflecting,
craving craving craving endlessly.

Without measure this this this horror!
who makes measure of value for value
is double damned
makes sickness of metaphor
confusion of tongues.
Lightning breaks tower
as counsel darkens.

Value is brilliantly borne aloft
in hot chariots
while glittering out of sky
hate falls on helpless wheat.

3.
Theory of value in itself
must then imply an economic scrutiny,
how an image differs from a thing.

Fluctuation of the dollar:
waving of linguistic formulas
in the wind of mind.

      IT IS THE VALUE MOVING

    the language of value / rational measure

              not rhythm

   or moving measure or mastery of time and fire
             that is alchemy.

SO,
  Value is of the excrementitious nature of Time (wch was sufficiently demonstrated in THE BURDEN OF SET #1, Appendix II, B). The self-realization of energy (13th Trump) in the autonomy of the visible is hindered by the cultsural holdon to European *humanitas,* that value-system that pinched us all. Come on, it's finished, Europe calling the dance, & Valéry should know. To each man, for use, what he has is given, & if he hasn't, well, it's being taken away from him, & pretty fast.

  Charles Ives writes, "…if a man finds that the cadences of an Apache war dance come nearest to his soul, provided he has taken pains to know enough other cadences — for eclecticism is part of his duty — sorting potatoes means a better crop next year — let him assimilate whatever he finds highest of the Indian ideal, so that he can use it with the cadences, fervently, transcendentally, inevitably, furiously, in his symphonies, in his operas, in his whistlings on the way to work, so that he can paint his house with them — make them a part of his prayer-book — this is all possible and necessary, if he is confident that they have a part in his spiritual consciousness."

We are in a rough time, the most difficult transition age of all, a real Interchange of Tinctures, where a kind of personal life is being exchanged for a kind of "universal." (What is not the person of an age is always experienced as "universe" by the new halfborn thing, the transition to, the baby with only his head sticking out of the vagina into his own time.)

It is the morning of the universal breath.

The old spectre of "greatness" in the arts, of a value-hierarchy into which every work of art (read *object of experience*) must be jammed, is a white spectre, & as the value of whiteness enantiodromically changes (like the suntan cult today as against that bleached ideal body of European middle age & renaissance), the systems of blackness toward which we are drawn arise. (The systems of blackness, the Ntu of Unison, seem chaos to receding whiteness, but will prove to be "system.")

European whiteness is sepulchre to us & European consciousness a museum.

"Those whose voices are accurate" (as Egyptian priests were called) do not attend to the curators of cultsure, the urbane caretakers. (If they get in the way we carve them with the Knife of Set.) It is not faith, or talk about, aurorals need, it is *that,* experience of. Then, what is to be attended, the substance of the new attentions, what is not disposable, is materials for the boat to make the crossing, & the tools, kosmanthropological.

As Olson said, "…the work of the morning is methodology," & the new attentions are bearing down.

2.   *"Nature" and the next 2000, give or take a few, years*

wha you say, "Nay-cher" ? wha you say, "Nay-cher" ?

I said gNature, "birth," prae-gnant
from (g)nasci, to be born. (I no say, "Gno……

It is born, the new Nature. & what we can say of it surely, though the surety is not our concern, is that it no longer is opposed to Another, a Super- or un-, not hung on, polarized to one of the swimming away from each other Fish. That polarity, that made it seem possible that anything unnatural (not to say Super-) could really occur, has gone away, & reality won't any more be divided between us & the world, the world (or God) getting the bigger share.

a few consequences

A.   Food

As control seems to increase, nature turning into human nature (or rather what before was "human nature" now understood as nature, Teilhard de Chardin's "interiorization" animistically exteriorized), food becomes politics, an FDA the central arm of government.

We are what we eat but turn it around, in the whole field (& think of flowers) no division between electricity, poison, medicine, food, drug, elixir. We cannot avoid absorbing microdilutions. All foods are drugs.

from the "Chapters of Coming Out by Day" :   "Tem hath built thy house, and the double Lion-god hath founded thy habitation; lo, drugs are brought, and Horus purifieth and Set strengtheneth, and Set purifieth and Horus strengtheneth."

B.   Wildlife & Permission

What was wildlife can't be any longer. An artificial wilderness is no wilderness, a national park is a National Park, in Africa or the moon. Danger does not make a wild life, you can permit danger in sport. Wild life is not game, can never be *permitted,* hunting & fishing are seasonally permitted, play.

It remains to be seen what cannot be permitted.

C.   The Sexual Image

All is permitted. Change in the Heavenly Female Power. As equality of sexes swings around, the biochemical basis of the old differentiation is shifted. This doesn't mean everyone will be "queer," but that as new magnetic centers astrally arise in men & women the scope of both amativeness & adhesiveness will be prodigiously enlarged.

****

1781.   the discovery of Uranus, who moves in a cycle
            of approx. 84 years, 7 years in each sign.

1862.   81 years later Ulrichs uses the word "Uranian,"
            after Plato's *Symposium,* referring to love of
            male for male

            Aquarius, toward which we move, is ruled
        by Uranus, according to contemporary astrologers,
        & ancient Greeks saw the sign as Ganymede.

Uranus dances with Ganymede on the heavenly floor.

****

In the fragments of Berosus, priest-historian, we can trace a Babylonian genesis from which was later derived both the Hebrew & the orphic (later, the Platonic) myths of the original bisexuality of the first man, Adam, male-female, from which the opposites were later separated & polarized by the male-female god.

Under the permissions, man will be able to find in woman more the original wholeness, & woman in man.

Marie Delcourt in *Hermaphrodite* shows the androgynous image of Classical times is a dream of a primordial union of male & female consciousness, closely linked with the vision of the bisexual Phoenix who perpetually renews himself in the fire of the morning of the Great Year.

The Work of the Renovating Intelligence.

Jesus said: "And if you make the male and the female one, so that the male is no longer male and the female no longer female, and when you put eyes in the place of an eye, and a hand in the place of a hand, and a foot in the place of a foot, and an Image in the place of an Image, then you will enter the Kingdom."

A.   Vision

   10997 B.C.   the negative afterimage of looking at the Sun was Man advancing bearing a water-jar

   1963 A.D.   the negative afterimage of the vision of Man poised in the electromagnetic currents of space is a roaring   Lion.

It is still hard to distinguish the form of the Lion, who walks
                                                           in flame.

The text of this book is set in Adobe Minion Pro
designed by Robert Slimbach with display
set in Matthew Carter's Mantinia.
Design and typesetting by
Jonathan Greene.